I0170454

A Strenuous Day

Wayne Mahood

Milne Library

Geneseo, NY

2015

© 2015 Wayne Mahood

978-1-942341-14-7 print

978-1-942341-15-4 ebook

Some Rights Reserved.

This work is licensed under a Creative Commons Attribution-NonCommercial-ShareAlike 3.0 Unported License.

You are free to:

Share—copy and redistribute the material in any medium or format

Adapt—remix, transform, and build upon the material

The licensor cannot revoke these freedoms as long as you follow the license terms.

Under the following terms:

Attribution—You must give appropriate credit, provide a link to the license, and indicate if changes were made. You may do so in any reasonable manner, but not in any way that suggests the licensor endorses you or your use.

NonCommercial—You may not use the material for commercial purposes.

ShareAlike—If you remix, transform, or build upon the material, you must distribute your contributions under the same license as the original.

Photos courtesy of the author, except where otherwise noted.

Published by Milne Library

State University of New York at Geneseo,

Geneseo, NY 14454

Acknowledgments

How does one truly recognize and thank all the persons who made this book come to pass? First, I thank the subjects, my grandparents, Harve and Harriette Claypool England, whose lives are chronicled and who left vital information about themselves. Certainly, I thank my mother, Ruth England Mahood, her brothers, Howell and Samuel England, sister Rachel England Palm and sister-in-law, Mildred Cooper England. Each provided countless documents and revealing memories.

Charlotte and William Brummett, whose reading of the manuscript and encouragement to test the waters as well as friendship mean more to me than they will ever know. Elizabeth Argentieri, who has been so very helpful over the too few years I've gotten to know her, saw the manuscript's potential and was the critical link to the publisher. Publishing Manager Allison Brown expertly and thoughtfully guided the process with a sure, but light touch, and student editor Sarah Smith, a very bright, senior English major, found materials overlooked and countless ways to express what I wanted to say.

Finally, as I've had to do too many times, I apologize to Bobbi for once more grumbling my way through a writing assignment.

Table of Contents

PREFACE VII

Prologue
The Clock 3

Chapter One
Missouri Beckons 5

Chapter Two
Quitman 21

Chapter Three
Maryville 31

Chapter Four
The Englands Make Their Mark 49

Chapter Five
The Transitional Years 63

Chapter Six
Harve Drops a Bombshell 77

Chapter Seven
The Englands Settle In 85

Chapter Eight
Velma Colter 99

Chapter Nine
"It Sure Was a Strenuous Day" 113

Chapter Ten
The Sheriff's "Trial" 127

Chapter Eleven
Starting Over 139

EPILOGUE 157

BIBLIOGRAPHY 161

INDEX 165

Preface

This is a very personal story, and one from which I was
sheltered well into adulthood. I'm not even sure when
I first became aware of the plot's outlines, but I became
engrossed in the lives of my grandparents when my mother
shared a diary her mother kept sporadically from 1919 to 1940.
An entry on January 12, 1931, stood out, as she wrote, "It sure
was a strenuous day"—a typical understatement. The events of
that day blackened her husband's name and her adopted city's.

Her diary, written on three by five inch notepads, is the
basis for this narrative. Harriette ("Hattie") and Harvey England
were transplanted Ohioans who found each other in the little settlement of Quitman in northwestern Missouri in the late 1880s.
Their parents, at least both of Hattie's, had hauled their families
to Quitman to start life anew. Harvey made the trek to Missouri
with just his father and sister.

It is unclear why Hattie's father, Byron Claypool, and her
mother, Elizabeth, came to Quitman by way of Illinois with ten
children. Nor is it clear how Byron, a Civil War veteran and
non-practicing lawyer, made a living—or intended to. They simply appeared to follow other Ohioans bent on changing their fortunes.

On the other hand, Harvey's father, Jesse, a Civil War
short-timer and farmer, was heartbroken over the loss of his
wife, Eliza Ann. Devoutly religious and always upbeat, Eliza Ann
had died shortly after delivering her fifth child. Only three of

her children, including Harvey, survived infancy. Jesse's sister- and brother-in-law, already in Quitman, had lured Jesse with the promise of greener pastures.

In time, Harvey and Hattie met there in Quitman. Then, older than most newlyweds at the time, they gave up their inde- pendence, on—of all days—Independence Day, 1900. Eighteen years later, they uprooted themselves and their four children and moved to Maryville, the county seat. While just some thirteen miles away, it was a world apart in terms of amenities and oppor- tunities. Things went as well as could be expected until Harvey's election as Nodaway County sheriff in 1928, which led to Hat- tie's "strenuous day."

Well, that's the story in outline. For most of my grandpar- ents' lives, their story was that of thousands of hardy souls who sought a better life in the rural Midwest. Yet ultimately, theirs was anything but an ordinary tale. When I first began my re- search, the Englands—my grandparents—were just players in a larger setting. As a rather new college faculty member, I saw their story as an academic challenge and focused on the events that dramatically changed their lives. My first forays were in- quiries to the Northwest Missouri State University Library and the editor of the *St. Joseph News Press*, who claimed firsthand knowledge of significant events in the 1920s and 1930s. Neither proved helpful. Then I turned to newspapers, which began pro- viding details. Finally, I turned to family—my parents, uncles, and aunts, who, though unusually quiet and circumspect, were more or less helpful. Over time, they unearthed letters, photos, scrapbooks, and newspapers. However, other interests and obli- gations intervened.

Sometime in the late 1970s, when my mother shared Hat- tie's notepads, I rediscovered an interest in my grandparents' lives. This led to my 1977 article about Hattie in the Nodaway County Historical Society's *Tales of Nodaway County*. But again, other activities interceded. Finally, with the deaths of my par- ents, the passing of my mother's siblings, and my pending retire- ment, I felt compelled to do something with my growing collec- tion of material.

The current emergence of memoirs and social histories was the final push I needed to complete my grandparents' story. Stories of individual lives are being used to reveal something about all of us, how we came to be, and what forces have shaped our individual and collective lives. Our pasts catch up with us in various ways. Most recently and dramatically, for instance, the Great Recession of 2008 called on us to look back to the Great Depression, from which we might learn coping mechanisms. Similarly, resurrecting the Englands' lives may provide insight into our own lives.

This is also about a formative era in the creation of modern America—the early twentieth century. It marked the advent of airplanes, radios, motion pictures with sound, and mass-produced cars. Americans experienced a modern day plague, a world war, a Great Depression, and when escaping from it all, sixty home runs in a season without the benefit of steroids. All were carefully recorded in Hattie's small notebooks, and as agents of cultural change, still resonate today.

At its core, this is a tale of two otherwise ordinary persons whose lives intersected with an historic set of events.

A Strenuous Day

Prologue

The Clock

I t was funny that I noticed the clock's strike. Most times I didn't. Or likely, I ignored it. But now, I got to thinking about earlier times I didn't hear it. Like those Christmas mornings when the clock seemed eerily hushed, and when my older cousin and I lay abed. No particular year stands out. Rather, it was waiting for the clock to signal time to get up, time to be surrounded by our extended family. They were noisy adults all trying to tell their stories—often at the same time.

Seven decades later, I can still remember that silent clock and the long nights up in that cold attic. Would morning and my release from that exile never come? Yes, there were things to do in the attic. I would rummage through all the items stored away, like the cow that mooed—a little toy that made the sound of a cow when tilted the right way. Tilting it a few times always satisfied.

More tantalizing was the revolver, hanging in a holster from one of the rafters. The stern admonition never to touch it resounded in my ears. Yet, there it was, irresistibly tempting. I stealthily crept over the floorboards, trying to muffle the sound. Warily, with one eye peeled toward the stairs, I imagined myself like my western hero Gene Autry—revolver in the palm of my hand, finger on the trigger, thumb poised to draw back the hammer. I would be the western gunslinger protecting the pretty schoolmarm in distress. But I dared not touch it. Harve England, the gun's owner and my grandfather, was too forbidding.

I couldn't get over why I wasn't allowed to play with the revolver. I was careful with my cap gun, and while the loud pop and burst of smoke might scare my dog, I never did any harm. Why was everyone so quiet when I asked about the revolver? Clearly, it was more than a firearm; there was something dark, secretive about it.

So, back to the mattress on the floor and waiting for the clock to announce reveille.

Would that clock ever strike? Minutes became hours. Hours, days. It was Hattie's clock—nothing special, just a mantel clock, one that Sessions made tons of. But, it was always known as the "jail clock."

Hattie, I later learned, had bought it from her sister Dora. Hattie had liked the clock, because it was a reminder of her sister. But, before long she came to dread hearing it strike. It had become a reminder of that day, of man's cruelty to man. It would haunt her, her husband, and their children. But she is long gone and so are they. If only the clock were gifted with a tongue—it could tell quite the story.

Chapter One

Missouri Beckons

It had never been easy for Hattie. Born Harriette Lamira Claypool, she was the second child and eldest daughter of a family of thirteen, twelve of whom lived to adulthood. She became the mother when her own mother, Elizabeth, died from typhoid fever. Actually, as the eldest daughter, Hattie was the surrogate mother even before her mother's passing. Taking care of such a large brood demanded two parents, and it's unclear what kind of parent her father Byron was. He made claims to being a lawyer, albeit a non-practicing one. Increasingly, he sat in a rocker reading, or in time, having a grandchild read to him. He preferred poetry by his favorite—and namesake—Lord Byron.

Byron Claypool was a native Hoosier, having been born in Morristown, Indiana, about twenty miles southeast of Indianapolis. After attending school in Lafayette, Indiana, and teaching there a couple of years, Byron had volunteered to serve in the Union Army in 1863. At age twenty-three, he was mustered as a sergeant in Company D, 116th Indiana Infantry, a six-month non-combatant outfit organized in Lafayette. In fact, the regiment was in only two engagements before being mustered out at the end of February 1864.

Just three years later, and shortly before marrying Elizabeth Graves, Byron read law with an Indianapolis lawyer and was admitted to the bar. However, as far as anyone knows, he never actually entered into practice. In fact, just how he fed his twelve children is a mystery. At best, Byron could have been called a farmer, although much of the money he had seems to have come from renting out his land, his Civil War pension, and contributions from various children's wages.

Poor Elizabeth, a woman eight years Byron's junior, delivered children with merciless regularity—ten between 1868 and 1883, when the Claypools moved to Toulon, Illinois. In 1884, Byron and Elizabeth packed up again, following the lead of other Ohioans, and moved to R.R.2, Burlington Junction, Missouri, just north of Quitman.

The Chicago, Burlington & Quincy (CB&Q) and the Wabash railroads would in time provide jobs for the older boys. Alongside the lure of employment, many were attracted by the mineral springs a mile and a half southwest of the little railroad junction. Locals, who had discovered it in 1881, claimed that the springs relieved aches and pains. Shortly, an enterprising resident opened the Mineral Springs Sanitarium, a combination sanitarium and hotel built to accommodate between fifty and sixty guests. However, the Claypools never availed themselves of the sanitarium.

As three more children were born to Elizabeth and Byron there in Quitman, increasingly the adolescent Hattie was expected to perform household chores. Then in 1892, just two years after the birth of her last child, Elizabeth was gone—taken by typhoid fever.

In her absence, Byron counted even more heavily on his twenty-two-year-old daughter. Unfortunately, the domineering Byron would have taxed the patience of Job. For the time, Hattie accepted her fate. Someone had to mother the eight children still under their roof. In fact, with help from her younger sisters, Dora and Dosia, she was caring for eleven. Brothers Spencer and Isaac were away working on the railroad for periods of time, but often returned for home cooking and a place to rest.

There was an old saying among Nodaway pioneers:

Man works from sun to sun,
But woman's work is never done.

It certainly applied to Hattie and other women of the time.

Harriette (Hattie) with her sister, Theodosia, left, and Dora, sitting

Waking in the dark morning hours, Hattie began her day by dressing with the help of a dim candle or small kerosene lamp. One of her first chores, assuming one of her brothers had fired up the kitchen stove, was getting breakfast for the family. In "the spider," a large cast iron pan, she often fried eggs brought in from the hen house, salt pork, and possibly even smoked ham from one of their hogs.

Customarily, Mondays were washday. To fill a copper washtub, water was hauled from the well and heated on the stove in a large iron kettle. Lye soap, made from wood ashes placed in a barrel, was then cut into small pieces and dumped into the washtub. After being scrubbed and beaten against the washboard, the clothes were hung on the line to dry, or freeze, depending on the season. The leftover lye water often would be used to make hominy from the white corn grown on some farms.

On Tuesdays, the newly clean garments were ironed. Hattie would stand by the kitchen stove and rotate three sadirons, with two at a time staying hot on the stove. It was no small task to iron the starched men's dress shirts or the ankle-length petticoats, skirts, and dresses. Keeping the iron bright and smooth meant periodically rubbing it with beeswax. When the film of homemade starch stuck to the iron's metal bottom, it was run over coarse salt sprinkled on paper. Meanwhile, Hattie or one of her siblings had to keep feeding logs, corncobs, or woodchips into the stove.

Often, the garden was also the woman's responsibility. This meant planting and hoeing the vegetables (beans, corn, potatoes, turnips, and carrots), later digging them up, and canning, drying, and storing them over the winter. Depending on the season, Hattie or her sisters would search the fencerows and woods for wild gooseberries, blackberries, and nuts. In the late summer and fall, they made apple, peach, or wild plum butter to spread onto bread slices.

Even with a father and brothers, Hattie and her sisters were not exempt from dressing rabbits, squirrels, and chickens. They never completely got over the wild gyrations of the bloody, headless chickens after they were decapitated by an axe. Then, after they had boiled the chickens and plucked the smelly feathers, the girls would either bake or fry the birds.

Eventually, Hattie could stand being the homemaker no longer and moved in with a neighbor known as Widow Bacon. She also got a job in a millinery store—the family needed the money.

Now a ghost town, Hattie's hometown once bustled—if it can be said that a town of 332 people could ever "bustle." In fact, the whole of Green Township had barely 700 inhabitants. It might never have existed without the Bilby Ranch. In 1856, old John S. Bilby had moved from his native New Jersey to Illinois. He had learned carpentry back home, and followed his trade for a few years. Then in 1868, he took up farming on a five-hundred-acre plot just four miles from Quitman. Before long he would own land in three adjacent counties as well as in four other states, including Texas.

The Bilby operation was grandly touted as a "self-sustaining unit," not unlike the company towns that sprang up around coal mines and factories. It included a general store, which extended credit to ranch workers until the close of the harvest; a blacksmith shop, where another set of workers shod horses, sharpened plow shears, and built and repaired wagons; a post office; a one-room school; a meat packing house; a mill to grind cattle feed; and a flour mill (for human feed, of course). Old John built a mill and three or four dwellings in town near the general store to house workers with families. He also built a boarding house to accommodate as many as forty unmarried workers at a time. He exemplified the legendary nineteenth-century entrepreneur. By the time he died from an accident at age eighty-seven, he was one of the largest landowners in the United States.

The operation was so large that the CB&Q Railroad built a spur, called the Kansas City, St. Joseph and Council Bluffs Railroad, just to haul cattle to and from the Bilby Ranch.

Where were we? Ah, yes, Hattie and the millinery store. The store was attached to Bilby's general store and just west of the blacksmith shop. Pretty little Rachel Smith (née England) worked there in the millinery store. Rachel, born just at the end of the Civil War, had married Bob Smith, handyman and owner of "R.H. Smith, Blacksmith" shop. Bob built a modest house just off the town's main street where they raised twin daughters. At the nearby church, Rachel played the organ and offered her clear, soprano voice to the choir.

Working at the millinery shop not only afforded Hattie some income and independence, but it also was where she met Harvey England, Rachel's younger brother. As far as Hattie knew, Harvey just happened to come in to see his sister. Though not inclined to be a matchmaker—Rachel was much too reticent to admit it—she had encouraged her brother to come by when Hattie was sure to be there. He needed someone like Hattie: feet on the ground, thoughtful, capable, and attractive.

Harvey had been drifting. He was lonely, but outwardly he seemed particularly self-sufficient.

In his early twenties, Harvey was just a shade under six feet tall, dark-haired, brown-eyed, and square-jawed, Years later, his younger daughter imagined him as John Wayne riding hell-bent for election into town: he would pull up short, casually throw his leg over the horse's mane, alight gently on the ground, and hitch his horse to the railing in front of the store. In this scene, Hattie would greet him with the requisite "Howdy, stranger, haven't seen you in these parts before. Reckon you'll stay a while?"

And it would be love at first sight. Well, that would be a good story too. But, John Wayne in a store, which sold women's hats? Or Hattie sounding like *Gunsmoke's* "Miss Kitty"? In truth, Harvey was more like Gary Cooper: "Yup," "Nope."

More likely, their meeting wasn't nearly so dramatic or romantic. They met all right, but nothing happened at first. Hattie was too shy and self-effacing. If anything, Hattie tried to hide from Rachel's brother, though she was curious.

Nonetheless, Harvey got a good look at Hattie and took interest. Her shyness made her more attractive. She was tall, slim-waisted (as the laws of fashion demanded), and had dark hair drawn up on her forehead. But Hattie would always see herself as plain. Almost thirty, she was considered an old maid. Moreover, she had her father and siblings to care for. Even if something developed with Harvey, she couldn't even think of abandoning her responsibilities.

Plus, Hattie didn't really know Harvey—there hadn't been much opportunity. Hattie had lived near Quitman for just the past five years. Harvey had been out West in Washington Territory, homesteading with his father, Jesse. Father and son had packed up and left Quitman—just like that.

It may be that Jesse had wanted to get away from Quitman. It may be that he just wanted to get away from it all. He still mourned the death of his beloved wife, Eliza Ann, back in Ohio. At just thirty-five years old, she had died only days after delivering baby Edward, succumbing to what everyone there referred to as "the sickness." Likely it was deadly milk sickness, which killed Nancy Hanks Lincoln, Abraham's mother, and seemed to strike so many in Ohio, Indiana, and Illinois then.

Deeply religious Eliza Ann had already lost one child, Mary Alice, who died almost immediately after birth. Still, she had Clarinda Jane, who was born when Eliza Ann was barely nineteen; Rachel, who came along six years later; and little Harvey, who arrived almost exactly three years after her. How Eliza Ann marveled at her Harvey and prayed that he would live to adulthood. He was one of her few joys, for life was tough for the Englands and their neighbors.

Jesse England, unknown date

Not that Eliza Ann and Jesse were complainers. They simply faced up to the problems that plagued them, including (as Eliza wrote an aunt), "the right smart of sickness of one kind or other" that afflicted them and their neighbors. While Eliza Ann's father had "been right weakly all summer," Eliza, Jesse, and their children had been "as well as common." Not even that awful July 1873, when three weeks of daily rains came close to wiping out the bountiful wheat and corn crops, daunted them. The corn, where it had not been knocked down by the bad storms, was drowned by the rains. Even so, Eliza Ann considered herself lucky. One of their neighbors had been killed by lightning while returning home from a big Independence Day celebration in town. It was just a reminder, she has written, that "we haven't got our lives in our own hands."

Having lost a child and experienced a neighbor's death, Eliza Ann was acutely conscious of her own mortality. Her belief in the hereafter provided comfort, and as she wrote to Jesse's sister and brother-in-law, Delilah and George Smith, she prayed that she would "meet them in Heaven should they die before we see each other again." She reflected, "we should live such a life that we should always be redy to die should we be caled on the road or at home or eny place else to die." Oh, how she wished they could meet her Harvey, who wanted his Uncle George to come visit him. At five years old, Harvey was already big, and Eliza Ann predicted that he "will make a stout man"—if he survived the sickness that was "very comon this time of the year." As was her habit, she ended the letter, "your friend untill Death."

That December, 1873, she wrote George and Delilah again to tell them that her family was well; in fact, everyone near Indian Creek was well. Eliza Ann had an almost mystical feeling for Indian Creek and its hold on the people who had lived nearby. She was convinced that once people had drunk its refreshing water, even if they moved as far away as Arkansas, they would always return. She also reported that there had been five or six weddings since she had last written, which counterbalanced the "great many Deaths this summer and fall."

As expected, prices were high because of the rains that summer: potatoes cost 60¢ to 75¢ a bushel, a dozen eggs cost 25¢ (the equivalent of approximately $6.00 in 2015), butter was 20¢ to 25¢ a pound, and money was scarce. Fortunately, Jesse had other ways to make a living. Even as Eliza Ann was writing, Jesse was busy in his shop making wooden barrels for storing lard. They were selling for $1.55 a piece, a decent price.

Jesse stopped his work long enough to write a postscript at the top of Eliza Ann's letter proudly proclaiming that his young son, Harvey, had been shooting his pop gun all evening. Jesse was proud of his son, who he felt was big—even for boys in Ohio. However, just over a month later, Jesse's holiday spirit was dampened by the "heaviest Sleet" he had ever seen. He lamented to his sister that it had broken nearly half of his timber and ruined the orchards he had worked so hard to cultivate. More than half of his fruit trees had been uprooted. Still, between the wheat he had harvested (in one of the most difficult harvests ever), the corn he had salvaged, and the thirty-five pork barrels which he would take over to Chillicothe to sell when the roads froze and were passable again, they would make out.

Despite the loss of income due to the low corn yield that summer, the loss of the fruit trees that winter, and the rising prices for goods, forty-two-year-old Jesse and thirty-four-year-old Eliza Ann considered themselves lucky at the beginning of 1874. The children were well and progressing at the local school. In fact, Clarinda Jane (Clara) was becoming quite the young woman. It wouldn't be long before she was married.

Though they did not know it then, before another year was out, six-year-old Harvey would have a baby brother. Another boy could be a real help on the farm.

On April 5, the very day she delivered baby Edward, Eliza Ann became ill. Jesse would long remember that sad time. Eliza Ann, confined to bed, had tried to retain her optimism. But two days later, she called Jesse to her bed and asked him to sit beside her. She told him that she would never get well and not to grieve after her, for she was ready to go. Then comforted by her faith, she told Jesse that she would meet him and all her friends in Heaven. In fact, Jesse wrote his sister- and brother-in-law, "My wife Eliza died happy and is gon to a Spirit world where i expect to meet her again."

While seemingly philosophical, he sorely missed Eliza Ann. Breaking a promise to her that he would stay in Indian Creek and keep the children with him, Jesse had placed baby Edward in the care of Eliza Ann's brother- and sister-in-law. The good news, he wrote sister Delilah, was that he had visited "my little Son Edward England," then eleven days old, and had found him well except for a sore mouth that was healing.

Then, to Jesse's dismay, tiny Edward too succumbed to disease and was buried next to his mother and Mary Alice, the sister he had never known. Jesse faithfully tried to keep the home and family together, at least for another four years. Clara was gone—she'd gotten married. So, it was just ten-year-old Rachel and seven-year-old Harvey. But it had been too much for him. His "pap" had died, the damaged orchards were not bearing fruit, and the timber had been reduced to the point that he could not mill enough to make barrels. Most of all, there were too many memories of his Eliza Ann. It was time to move on, to leave her beloved Indian Creek. His sister Delilah and Missouri beckoned.

Delilah's husband, George, had been importuning Jesse to come out to Quitman as far back as 1869. George had written that no one could hire him to come back and live in Ohio again. Land was cheaper near the Nodaway River, his apple orchard was the pride of the area, and there was nothing that could not be grown there in Quitman. Perhaps most importantly, there was plenty of work for the willing.

With hope for a new beginning, Jesse sold his farm, gathered Rachel and Harvey, and packed up his few belongings. Maybe, as his wife had professed, he would return to her Indian Creek. Maybe.

As George had written, the town of Quitman was growing—slowly at best, but growing. There were now 335 hardy souls living in the village and another 2,500 living in the township. Good farmland was available, and it was only thirteen miles from Maryville, the county seat. Three miles to the north lay Burlington Junction, a railroad depot through which trains from two of the Midwest's main railroads, the CB&Q and the Wabash, crossed.

While the West called thousands, the northwestern Missouri town of Quitman seemed to be a particular magnet for Ohioans. They came in droves to Nodaway County, beginning as early as 1843, when a fellow named Jackson surveyed the land and staked out farms for his Buckeye friends. Soon they drove the Pottawatomie Indians away and took whatever farmland they could lay their hands on. In fact, before long there was a settlement (now long gone) called "Old Xenia" and a little cemetery between Quitman and Burlington Junction known as "Ohio Cemetery." One of the first county sheriffs, who lived to the ripe old age of one hundred, was an Ohioan, as was one of the first doctors and first blacksmiths.

African Americans were also drawn to the area, some brought as slaves by Kentuckians and Tennesseans, and others enjoying their new-found, post-Civil War freedom. The area's ballyhooed fertile soil, so important to agriculture and animal raising, was attractive to those seeking something better. However, as late as 1930 the black population never exceeded 250.

Shortly after the Civil War, the growth of Nodaway County was marked by subscriptions to build a railroad, following the Hundred and Two River (familiarly the 102 River), through Maryville. There are various explanations for the name given the river, which is a tributary of the Platte River. One explanation is that it was 102 miles from the Mormons' previous camp on their trail to Utah. Another is that Brigham Young told his followers that it was the 102nd river they had crossed getting there from Nauvoo, Illinois. Or it could be a translation of the French Riviere Cent Deux. Whatever one believes, the river is as unpredictable as its name is unusual—it barely flows at times, while at other times it floods.

By 1880 there were five separate railroads running through the county, connecting it with Kansas City to the south, and all the way through Iowa and Illinois to Chicago.

By the time Jesse, Rachel, and Harvey arrived in Quitman, there were mills down on the Nodaway River, which ground corn for the hogs being raised in increasing numbers. Hogs and cattle abounded where, according to local legend, buffalo once roamed. Importantly, the valley proved fertile for a rich variety of crops, including corn, onions, and asparagus. Orchards bore a wide variety of apples, especially Golden Grimes, a particular favorite. Of course, that meant cider in the fall, and if stored long enough in their cellars, vinegar. Eventually, bluegrass too would become a marketable crop.

In the summer of 1879, Jesse, Rachel and Harvey set up housekeeping. Harvey was big enough to take on more chores, and even hire himself out to make extra money. However, he was distracted by playing ball whenever he got a chance. This was especially true on summer Sundays, when the town baseball team would play, typically a doubleheader. Harvey already had his sights on becoming a member of the team.

However, barely four years later Jesse wanted to move again. Daughter Clara was living with her husband, Will, and their family outside Spokane in Washington Territory. In her letters, she extolled the merits of the land there. Land was cheap and plentiful, deer were abundant, and the rivers were crystal clear. Jesse and Harvey could fish to their heart's content. Well, why not? Daughter Rachel had found a good man—gentle, thoughtful Bob Smith would take care of her.

Slim, dark-haired, and broad-shouldered, Bob Smith was one of the twelve blacksmiths descended from old James Wallin Weddle, who set up the first shop in Quitman. Bob learned to do most everything in the Weddle's busy shop before he set off on his own. In fact, he thrived on challenges to his ingenuity. He had previously patented a machine that cut off bluegrass heads and sacked the seeds. He even built a car. This was some time later, around 1898, but before Ford patented his "horseless carriage." Bob simply applied his blacksmithing and bicycle-making skills to create a self-propelled carriage. It had two huge wheels attached in the front, to which a chain was connected, which in turn propelled the carriage. But, strangely, he and his partner J.J. Gillinger never patented their design.

Anyway, in 1884 Jesse sold his small farm and headed west with sixteen-year-old Harvey. Jesse claimed that it was for his health, but he was also restless and lonesome. He still missed his Eliza Ann, and wanted to see his older daughter Clara.

At the end of August, Jesse dutifully wrote his daughter Rachel that he and Harvey stood the trip to Washington Territory with a whole carload of migrants tolerably well. They had landed in a place called Peone Prairie, near Spokane. Nearby Medical Lake, which teemed with fish, had lured Harvey almost immediately upon their arrival.

One had to be self-sufficient out there, and Harvey proved especially so. Though weighing only 130 pounds, Harvey was nearly as tall as his father and becoming quite handy. In addition to the usual farming chores, he learned how to raise fruit trees. He was also proving a skillful hunter, often putting venison on the table. In fact, he was learning to butcher, render the fat into lard, make sausage, and tan hides.

Rachel England Smith, Harve England's sister

On the other hand, though outwardly healthy, red-cheeked Jesse was not quite as capable. He had never fully recovered from an enlarged heart, which had led to his discharge from the 89th Ohio Regiment in 1863 after less than a year's duty during the Civil War.

Like Hattie's father's, Jesse's military experience was without honors. In fact, he had contracted pneumonia at Camp Dennison, Ohio, barely two months after he enlisted. Though twenty-seven-year-old Jesse returned to duty, he was never well, and from March to June 1863 he was in the Nashville, Tennessee, State Hospital No. 1. He was then transferred to the Louisville, Kentucky, Hospital No. 13 until his discharge in July. On the other hand, Jesse could consider himself lucky. He had escaped the bloody Battle of Chickamauga in November 1863. Still, due to his illness his discharge papers indicate that he was "unable to perform manual labour the greater part of [his] time." Nonetheless, he had been able to make a passable living since then as a cooper and sometime farmer.

So the Englands, father and son, tried to make a new life for themselves. Yet, barely a year later, Jesse wanted to return to Quitman. He would have, he claimed, if he had had the money—but he couldn't seem to raise any crops. He was unsettled. Maybe he would try the Columbia River area, where Harvey was thriving and showing his growing independence.

Fifteen months later, in December 1886, Jesse was even more despondent. Lumbering, which paid 25¢ an hour, had come to an end when bad weather blocked the deeply rutted roads. He had set up housekeeping with his pal James Burgess, and they warmed themselves by the No. 8 Stove Jesse purchased for five dollars. They could make it by cutting wood, getting a dollar a cord. Happily, the two had recently cut ten cords. So, Jesse wrote his daughter Rachel that he might be satisfied if he had someone to cook for him.

He vacillated. One day he would be up, as up as he ever was. The next, he didn't even care whether he lived or died. His crippled hip made it difficult to sit for long, and he missed Harvey, who had been up to see him only once in the past six months.

While gone in the Columbia River area, Harvey had been married and divorced. He may have just wanted to be with a woman—someone who could love him. Maybe he really wanted a mother; his mother had passed when he was so young. Still, it was foolish of him to have married. The less said, the better, he figured, and for all intents and purposes, that was the end of the matter.

Now, Harvey was restless too—on the move, looking for satisfying work. He tried Seattle, on the coast, then Kalama, up river from Portland, Oregon. He liked that part of the territory, especially the salmon, about which he wrote his father in hopes of convincing him to relocate. Still following work, Harvey got hired to help build a railroad bridge at Scio, Oregon, just northeast of Corvallis. There, he cut his foot badly. While mending, he had too much time on his hands and too little money.

Jesse had thought about joining Harvey. In one letter, he had even tried to entice daughter Rachel and her husband Bob to come to Washington and "make a home with" them. His first inducement was the beautiful weather. If they came out, they would never go back to Missouri, where the wind blows all the time. Deer were plentiful, and the government land commissioner had made available 250,000 acres retrieved from the Northern Pacific Railroad. There was more than enough land for Rachel and Bob. Jesse even tried bribes. Earlier, Bob had asked how much he would have to pay for enough buck deer hide to make a pair of pants. The answer was $2.50, Jesse wrote Rachel, but if Bob came out there to live, Jesse would "give Bob a nuff to make him pants, vest coat, Socks and over coat free of charge." Finally, Jesse needed Rachel to mend the three or four pairs of his pants demanding repair. Jesse could do the washing and cooking all right, but not mend pants.

Elder daughter Clara wrote her sister that she had tried to accommodate "Pa," who complained that he was tired of staying on his ranch alone. (Apparently his partner had left.) Though slowly recovering from a vague illness that made it difficult for her to walk even a couple of blocks, she let her father move in with her family on a farm nearby, which seemed to satisfy Jesse— until a calamitous night in November 1888.

It was a Saturday night and there was a dance in town. Harvey, having returned to western Washington, hitched up his brother-in-law's team so sister Clara could accompany him to the dance. On the way, the horses got away from Harvey. Clara was thrown from the wagon, struck her head, and died almost immediately, leaving husband Will a widower with two small children. Harvey would never get over it, never mention Clara's name again. Nor would he ever be comfortable around horses again. Truth be told, he would never want to drive anything again— cart, wagon, or horseless carriage.

Jesse and Harvey, the heartbroken pair, were done with Washington Territory. They would go back "home"—Quitman, that is.

Chapter Two

Quitman

Once back in Quitman, Jesse and Harvey settled down in a little house on a narrow strip of land north of the village between the Nodaway River and the Kansas City, St. Joseph, and Council Bluffs Railroad.

At age twenty-one, Harvey had to start all over again and find a way to make a living. He took stock—he was industrious and resourceful. Homesteading had done that for him. Before long, he was hired to work on the large Bilby ranch nearby, and in time, he would attend auctions and bid on cattle for them. But first, he was assigned to do the "cowboy" chores: putting the cattle out to pasture, rounding them up, and installing fences to contain them.

The barbed wire that Joseph Glidden, an Illinois farmer, had patented fifteen years earlier was only slowly coming into use. For the most part, the prickly Osage orange, hauled in by the carload, was still the rancher's choice for fencing. Planted a foot apart, its thorny branches eventually intertwined so densely that not even a bird could fly through it. It was perfect there in Missouri, where trees for posts were not as abundant as in parts of the East. Once wire became more common, Harvey and his fellow "cowboys" strung it on the Osage orange "posts." Barbed wire was a must to contain cattle.

While Harvey worked hard, he still found time to indulge his love of baseball. The first year back in town, it seemed that he would never be accepted into the Quitman town team. But he made it, no doubt in part because of his imposing size.

Though Jesse did not approve of such foolishness, there wasn't much he could say. Harvey was his own man, and before long, he captained the team. In one doubleheader, he pitched the first game and caught the second, a success which Harvey proudly recorded next to a photo of him and his teammates:

Game: Maitland vs. Quitman
Batteries 1st game: England, Wright and Bird
Final score: Quitman 14, Maitland 8
Batteries 2nd game: Wright, Bird and England
Final score: Quitman 15, Maitland 9
Captain England

If he hadn't met and married Hattie, he probably would have played town ball forever. At least until his legs gave out. The legs always go first, you know.

Harve England (white shirt) with Quitman baseball team

It's not clear whether he played against any Maryville teams, including Maryville's "colored teams"—mainly the Black Bombers, whose fortunes over the years depended on the skills of the organizers. African Americans could play in pickup games, but not on the same team with whites. To find competition, the Black Bombers sometimes had to travel to Omaha.

Meanwhile, Harvey had been initiated into the Independent Order of the Odd Fellows, which met on the upper floor of the Select School on Quitman's main street. The symbol of this international fraternal organization, which dated to medieval times, was three interlocking rings, representing friendship, love, and truth. Harvey saw membership as a way to make friends, typically lifetime ones.

Still, sister Rachie knew that Harvey needed something more, *someone* more. So, she set up the meeting between her brother and her friend Hattie at the millinery shop. Like most, Hattie's and Harvey's courtship had its ups and downs, though it would have been difficult for the casual observer to tell. Neither was very expressive.

Their long, sporadic courtship was as problematic as Harvey's attempts to get letters to Hattie. During a trip for the Bilbys in March 1898, he wrote to his "Dear Friend" to explain his lack of correspondence. However, when he stuck his hand in a coat pocket later, he realized that he hadn't sent it. Another time he wrote from the Bilbys ranch and entrusted a letter to an old man who was carrying ten other letters written by ranch workers. The old man had dropped the letters in the mud and returned them to the writers. Harvey's explanation may have been a way of rationalizing his dilatory correspondence, or just filling space, for the remainder of the letter was quite short and mundane. However, Hattie seems to have accepted the explanations in the proper spirit, as she carefully saved his letters.

Neither was young anymore. Harvey was already thrity-two, and Hattie, a year his junior, was past the usual marrying age. By her lights, she was just, well, Hattie. But, there's no mistaking it, Hattie had plenty of backbone and was nobody's fool.

Though Hattie and Harvey had known each other for more than a decade, they didn't marry until July 4, 1900. There was something ironic about them marrying on Independence Day: two independent souls agreeing to a union, which would deny them their independence. Yet, they managed to maintain their autonomy in various ways. Hattie recorded her inner thoughts in brief diary entries. Sporadically she would write a few paragraphs each night, more often than not poking fun at herself. She also poked fun at those she considered stuffed shirts or know-it-alls.

Harvey maintained his independence through his work and membership and leadership in various community organizations. He would always be his own man, at times contrary to what Hattie might want. Though he socialized, he pretty much kept his thoughts to himself.

That fateful Independence Day Hattie was in her finest. Her Aunt Eliza Graves had made the wedding dress, while their businessman-friend Charley Turner supplied her ring and a ring on the belt of her dress. Reverend West officiated at the 6:00 p.m. ceremony in Widow Bacon's house, where the newlyweds and Harvey's father immediately took up their residence. There is no way of knowing why they stayed with her, except that apparently she had room for them. The Widow prepared a meal for the foursome, which included raspberry pie. Thus began the England's custom of annually serving raspberry pie on the Fourth of July.

The newlyweds bought their first furniture on credit, though it may well be the only time they ever did. And, characteristically, there was nothing extravagant about their purchases from Brown Brothers over in Maryville, Nodaway County's largest city. Harvey neatly inscribed the expense in his account book:

> 1 picture $1.00, 1 rocker $3.00, 1 mattress $3.00, 1 couch $20.00, 1 safe (kitchen cupboard) $8.00, spring for mattress $3.50, 1 set of chairs $6.50.

The total of $45 was to be paid back at $5 per month. While that might well have been almost 10 percent of Harvey's annual wages, he and Hattie extinguished their debt a full three months before the deadline. Above all else, debt was to be avoided—nothing would be worse than to end up in the county poor house.

However, it was not the first time Harvey had borrowed money. Back in December 1883, fifteen-year-old Harve had gotten himself into a scrape. He had gone to Fairbury, Nebraska, and needed ten dollars to get home by train. He had tried to borrow it, but the would-be lender backed out. So, stranded some 140 miles from home, "in the dogondest place ever I struck," Harvey anxiously wrote his brother-in-law Bob Smith: "Send me the money please and I will come back...send it right away." In return, Bob could have a "lean on my gun untill I pay it." He closed the letter with the plea, "don't tell my folks," and repeated himself, apparently for emphasis: "Send me the money and oblige. Harvey England." We have to figure that Bob complied.

The year 1900 was an exciting time to marry. Despite reminders that the new century did not begin officially until January 1, 1901, most looked forward to good times. Some looked back on the inventions of the previous century: steam engines, transcontinental railroads, ocean liners, the telegraph and telephone, electric lights, the cash register, and x-ray machines. These inventions transformed the world—travel time was cut dramatically, voices were transmitted over distances, houses were electrified, photography was revolutionized by a black box called a Kodak, and Pepsi Cola was created by a North Carolina pharmacist.

The upcoming year seemed particularly propitious: a bumper crop of corn was expected in the Midwest, and prices for goods were down about three percent over the past half dozen years.

Kansas's Carrie Nation was hatcheting liquor bottles to proclaim the prohibitionist message. Incumbent President William McKinley eagerly anticipated another four years with a new vice president, Theodore Roosevelt—the ebullient New York Governor and Spanish-American War hero, who had unexpectedly agreed to be his running mate. McKinley had again beaten William Jennings Bryan, "The Commoner," who had excited the folks in Quitman when he paid them a campaign visit in 1898. That rally was one of the biggest events the residents could ever recall.

While consumption, pneumonia, and diarrheal diseases were still the major causes of death in Missouri, generally the health of its citizens—and the nation—was improving.

Quitman's population had grown almost seven percent over the past decade, rising from 332 to 356, and the economy was starting to improve. The Bilbys kept expanding their operations, and Harvey's duties would increase proportionately. Beyond his growing duties at work, there would be greater responsibilities at home, including a boy, Jesse Howell, born in February 1902.

Harvey doted on the boy, affectionately called Howell (later and more commonly, "J.H."). He hated to leave his son when he had to go away on business. However, less than two months after Howell was born, Harvey had to go on a trip to Kansas City for the Bilbys. On the way there, Harvey wrote Hattie a "few lines" apologizing for not writing sooner, but he hadn't had the time. At 7:00 a.m. he and his partners had arrived in Maitland and immediately went to the stockyards, staying until 3:00 p.m. Then he went to the Shooting Park to watch the marksmanship contests before turning in for the night. The next morning, Harvey added in his letter that he had checked out Rosse's store, where he bought dress material for Hattie. He thought it was a "nice thing," and the owner claimed it "the best in the store at 85¢ a yard." Then once again he headed out to the stockyards, where he and his partners looked over cattle for the Bilbys.

At about 5:00 p.m. the next day, Harvey and his partners boarded the train for Kansas City and arrived just in time for supper. He sat down in the "Absolutely Fire Proof" New Coates Hotel to write, while his partners sat chatting, smoking, and debating about going to a movie show. Plans were to be home that Friday night with three train cars of cattle and maybe the thousand head he intended to bid on.

Harve wrote that Kansas City was a very pretty town, which he might come to like if it was not so noisy. He hadn't slept any. More importantly, Harvey badly missed Hattie and the baby. He ended his letter by promising to be home Friday night, or else he would write again, and signed off simply with "good Bye, Harvey." Although Harvey was not fond of endearments, there was no mistaking his affection for his wife and son.

Despite his hectic schedule, Harvey managed to build a wood frame house for his growing family, which still included Jesse. Three more children were born to Harvey and Hattie in quick succession: Samuel Herman in 1904, Ruth Delilah in 1908, and Rachel Elizabeth in 1910. Sam was named for Sam Rodman, a friend of Hattie and Harvey and the oldest man in Quitman. He had celebrated the Fourth of July at the Frankum ranch, where each lady tried to honor him with a piece of cake. Poor Sam obliged, overate, and quietly died in his sleep. The younger Sam hoped he would experience a similar fate. Ruth's name was familial: a combination of Hattie's youngest sister and Harvey's Aunt Delilah. And of course, Rachel's namesake was Harvey's pretty little sister.

England children (J.H., Ruth, Samuel) ca. 1909

Before baby Ruth was two, the three eldest England children had posed for an itinerant photographer. The two dark-haired, brown-eyed boys wore knickers, long black socks, high-buttoned shoes, white shirts, and large cravats. With serious faces, they stood on either side of their plump baby sister, Ruth, who was clad in a pretty white dress and watched the photographer intently. At about the same time, Howell's first day of school was recorded for posterity. As a first grader, he sat in the front row of Miss Lulu Parshall's young charges, three of which, befitting the times and possibly their status, were barefooted. At least Howell had his high-buttoned shoes and a starched and laboriously-ironed white shirt, which seemed mandatory for such special occasions.

Hattie and Harvey made sure their four children were well fed, clothed, and educated. Maybe the latter stemmed from their own spotty schooling. After all, Hattie had moved so many times. At about the same age her Howell was starting school, she moved from Ohio to Illinois, and at fourteen, she had moved again. By then, she had already taken on family responsibilities that made it impossible to attend school with any regularity. Harvey's lack of formal education was similar. Hattie and Harvey had attended the proverbial "school of hard knocks" and wanted something better for their children.

While their children's schooling was important to them, nationally barely half of white children between the ages of five to nineteen attended schools at this time, and only a third of African American children were enrolled. High school enrollment was even lower, with fewer than eleven percent of fourteen- to seventeen-year-olds in school. Hattie and Harvey would make sure their children were not only educated, but better educated than most of their peers.

Before long, Harvey decided that they needed a larger house and built (what was to them) a spacious white frame home up the hill. He and Hattie had their hands full, especially with Harvey's father, whose health was failing fast. Eighty-four-year-old Jesse, never really healthy, was by July 1914 an invalid, and two years later had become completely bedridden. Bright's disease, an acute and chronic inflammation of the kidneys, was now complicated by arteriosclerosis and gangrene of the left foot and leg. In addition to taking care of her four children and terminally ill father-in-law, Hattie still found herself having to accommodate her own domineering father (for example, writing letters for him and answering his imperious commands).

Jesse's decline was also hard on the England children. Jesse was moved to what had been the dining room. Howell, Sam, Ruth, and Rachel were admonished not to disturb him by passing through the room. In fact, to go upstairs to the two rooms they occupied, they had to climb a ladder and crawl over a small roof. It was an adventure for the two boys, but scary to six-year-old Rachel.

Then, in mid-October 1916, Jesse lay in a casket in the dining room. As the neighbors paid their respects, fourteen-year-old Howell looked at his white-haired, goateed grandfather and remembered his favorite expression: "Great patience alive!" Howell never knew exactly what he meant, but the phrase stuck.

Though never really close to him, losing his father was painful for Harvey. To make matters worse, he now had to come up with $216 for burial expenses. Doc Hindman wanted almost $20. J.W. Praisewater, the undertaker, asked for $136. The minister was paid $5. Burial clothes cost $8, the marker added another $45 and miscellaneous expenses amounted to $2. Unable to come up with that much, Harvey applied for reimbursement for a veteran's funeral from the federal government. After the usual paper work and delays, it was paid.

Shortly, Maryville beckoned. It was the county seat, thirteen miles southeast of Quitman, and had close to five thousand residents, including 118 African Americans, many of whose families had resided there since after the Civil War. Maryville could even claim a Missouri governor. Albert P. Morehouse, a Democrat, had succeeded to the office on the death of Governor John S. Marmaduke in 1889.

Unlike Quitman, Maryville had some paved streets, going back to 1900, which had brought on heated objections from those who didn't see the need (or didn't want to pay the assessments). Despite their protests, the first eight blocks of twenty-four-foot pavement, laid on four-inch concrete and mixed by hand, soon encircled the town square and extended out in all directions. Maryville residents also enjoyed brick or flagstone sidewalks, completed shortly after the street paving, and of course, after another round of disagreements. Paved streets were a real luxury, as they cut the ever-present dust in the summer and prevented ankle-deep mud after rains. However, residential areas would not have brick streets for years to come.

For a time, though, traffic was primarily borne by horse and wagons, necessitating stables. Nine bore such whimsical names as the "Star Barn," "The Palace," "Pike's Peak Livery," and "McJimseys." The last was owned by old man McJimsey, who seemed to have been in Maryville forever. Nearby there were harness shops and blacksmith shops. Old timers could remember eight blacksmiths located on or near the square. One was operated by the Baker boys, members of an established black family

The greatest inducement to relocate may have been Hattie's and Harvey's friends who, in increasing numbers, were moving to Maryville. Their good friend Warren Jones, who had apprenticed in Quitman and married just three years before the Englands, now operated a drug store on the town square in Maryville.

Generally, Maryville meant more opportunities. As the county seat, it was almost ten times as large as Quitman. It offered more ways to make a living, more and better schools, and a large variety of shops, including grocery, department, and hardware stores. Maryville claimed Dale Carnegie (*How to Win Friends and Influence People*) and author and screenwriter Homer Croy. Later luminaries were Sarah Caldwell, born in Maryville and first female conductor at the Metropolitan Opera, and teachers college graduate Henry Iba, who guided the Oklahoma State University basketball team to two consecutive NCAA championships. To Harvey and Hattie it seemed clear—there were more opportunities for them to improve their lives and their four children's.

In January 1917, on the frosty yet sunny day that marked Ruth Delilah's ninth birthday, the Englands uprooted themselves from Quitman, Hattie's and Harvey's home for almost thirty years and the birthplace of their four children. It was not a decision made lightly.

Chapter Three

Maryville

That frosty January morning, Hattie was in charge. Harvey had gone ahead with their dog Boods, driving the team pulling the wagon full of their household goods. Not surprisingly, there was some fussing from the four youngest children, which Hattie put up with in her no nonsense, yet understanding, fashion. The girls, mostly Ruth, were to help Hattie load suitcases and anything else they could carry on the CB&Q. They boarded two days later, riding the three miles to Burlington Junction before transferring to the Maryville line. Howell and Sam had been instructed to walk Rose, their milk cow, the thirteen miles to Maryville.

The boys, fifteen and thirteen respectively, unhappily plodded along the narrow road, occasionally getting out of the way of the wagons, the few cars, and even fewer trucks passing by. They made it to Bovard Corner, a little over halfway, when Rose— already slowing up—decided that was as far as she could go. Howell and Sam poked, pulled, pushed, and used some words that their parents probably were unaware they knew—to no avail. She simply wouldn't take another step. They argued for a while, with Howell reminding his brother that "Dad said take Rose to Maryville," and Sam countering, "I don't care what Dad said, that's it. Rose stays here." Ultimately, they decided to leave Rose with a farmer, who said he would keep her in his barn. The two then hoofed it the rest of the way without their charge, dreading what their father would say.

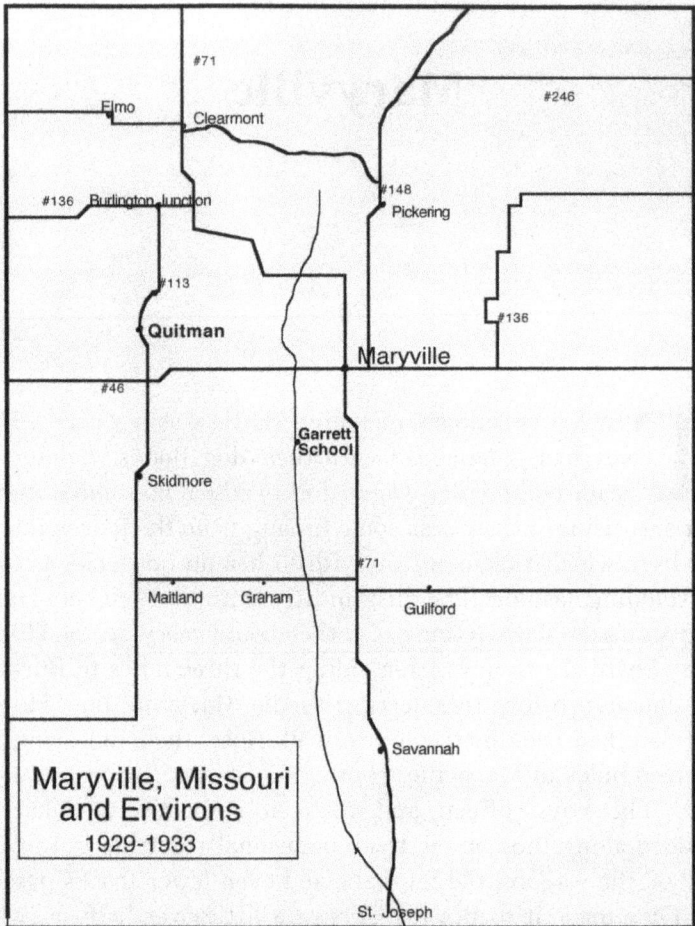

#71

Elmo
Clearmont

#246

#136 Burlington Junction

#148
Pickering

#113

Quitman

#136

Maryville

#46

Garrett
School

Skidmore

#71

Maitland   Graham

Guilford

Savannah

**Maryville, Missouri
and Environs**
1929-1933

St. Joseph

Map of Maryville, Missouri and Environs

Their father could be a forbidding figure. No, not really forbidding—stiff, reserved, even distant. Hattie would often admonish, "Don't let your Dad see you do that." Simply, he expected good behavior—and got it. Once, tiring of a grandson running around, Harvey calmly said to his daughter, the boy's mother: "It's time for him to be in bed." Like many a wife, Hattie sometimes kept him in the dark about certain matters. Not because she or their children were afraid of him—he never struck them, never threatened them, nor was he cranky, like his own father. It was just the way they were with each other. Truth is, his daughters remembered Harvey as tenderhearted *on the inside*. Hattie, soft outside, was tough *inside*.

It seemed to Howell and Sam that even without Rose, they would never get to Maryville. They had been there before—by train a few times and in the wagon—but never walking. It was bitter cold, so they stopped a few times to warm themselves at an inviting farmhouse. Actually, they stopped more than a few times, but knew they had to keep going. They kept looking for the Water Tower, Maryville's most famous landmark.

Like a sentinel, the great brick structure on iron stilts seemed to loom over the town. Similar to most towns in the Midwest, there was no high ground on which to put a reservoir. So, the resourceful Missourians built the tower into which water was pumped from the 102 River. Over time it had become a city landmark. Families picnicked near its base, and adventurous boys climbed the iron ladder, marking their courage with a piece of chalk and daring others to outdo them.

Old timers remembered when the tower had created an excitement of its own. Ice, tons of it, had formed at the top, and one warm spring day, with a roar, a tremble, and a dizzying rocking, the tower crashed to the ground, spewing water into the streets and homes nearby. It had been rebuilt and now appeared too stable to experience an encore. Right then, Howell and Sam were only interested in it as a marker to help them find their new home and warm themselves.

The weary England boys arrived in the early evening, relieved to find the little, one-story white house on the mostly empty south edge of town. Their father accepted their explanation for the absence of Rose, but made it clear that they next morning they would retrace their steps to retrieve her. He then let them warm themselves by the kitchen stove, eat some supper, and go to bed.

The next morning, another cold one, Howell and Sam retraced their steps to retrieve Rose. Upon their return—this time with Rose—Harvey took the boys up town to Corwin-Murrins clothing store, where he bought them new trousers, albeit yellow-toned ones, to look presentable their first day of school. Likewise, after they arrived by train, Hattie bought school clothes for the girls.

In time the four younger ones developed a routine. After they took turns washing from pans of water heated on the wood stove, doing their chores, and eating breakfast, the four headed off to school. Ruth and Rachel buttoned up for the seven-block walk to Garfield School, serving first through third graders in the southernmost ward of Maryville. A bit reluctantly, but dutifully, Howell and Sam escorted them and tried to calm their fears. Maryville seemed so much larger than Quitman. Previously they had all attended the same school; now they were going to be separated for the first time. After bidding their sisters goodbye, the boys walked another two blocks north and four east to the two-story, red-brick Washington School, the second of three to bear that name. Though a much longer walk to school than they were used to, they had to admit the paved streets made the walking easier.

Better yet, it was easy to find their way: north-south streets bore the names of trees, and many of the east-west streets were presidents. The major exceptions were the numerical streets beginning at the town square and running north.

Despite their age differences, Howell and Sam were both assigned to the eighth grade, Howell in 8A and Sam in 8B. School authorities ruled that rural Quitman schooling could never be comparable to Maryville's.

Though the boys were yet unaware, the school authorities also oversaw a "colored school" another five blocks east at the corner of East Jenkins and South Water streets. Except for a six-month period in 1881, when there were fewer than ten students, it had operated since 1870.

Of the approximately 155 black residents in the county, about 118 lived in Maryville, with the rest living mostly in small out-of-town settlements. Most of the black population held low income jobs, and worked variously as domestics, yardmen, coachmen, basket makers, farm laborers, barbers, janitors, shoe repairmen, caterers, and launderers. The general opinion among the white community was that they were dependable. The funeral for one black man who had been a bank's janitor for approximately forty years was heavily attended, and the bank manager served as one of the ushers.

Beginning in 1870, Missouri school law provided for segregated, but equal schools for African American children. School law also prescribed that the building, eventually to be constructed on the southeast part of Maryville, had to be to the same standard as the white school. Thirty-nine students, the largest ever, began their schooling in a rented building. Shortly a regular building, named Douglass (likely for Frederick Douglass), welcomed the students. After a fire destroyed the building in 1920, Maryville voters approved a five thousand dollar bond for a replacement.

Enrollment fluctuated and teachers came and went, with a married couple, Earnest and Mildred Boone, serving the longest. The students' names reflected the families that had been in Maryville virtually from the opening of the first school. For example, between 1916 and 1926 there were fourteen children named Gunn. Six were the children of Emmett and Mamie Gunn, and the great-grandchildren of Violet Gunn.

Violet's account of the Gunn family, one of the largest and best known black families in Maryville, is a fascinating oral history. She came as a slave from North Carolina with her baby Susan around 1861. Helped by a Missouri militiaman, she ran away from her master after they arrived in nearby Holt County. Then, the family of Dr. B.G. Ford gave her a ten-acre farm east of Maryville, which she later purchased with earnings as a domestic. She was married three times, first to Sam Gunn, who was "sold south." After her second husband, Susan's father, died, she remarried Sam Gunn, who by then had a son Sam. In turn, son Sam married Violet's Susan in 1868.

Daughter Susan and husband Sam had two daughters— one of whom was murdered in Omaha—and six sons, including Gilbert Emmett "Em" Gunn, a farm worker who lost a finger in a corn drill in 1893. Emmett and his wife Mamie had eight children, the oldest of whom was Raymond Gunn.

Despite some claims to the contrary, segregation extended to other educational activities. In 1921, a white student from Maryville named William Jewell was not allowed to represent Missouri in an oratorical contest because a contestant from Iowa was African American. Even Oak Hill Cemetery originally was segregated, but over the years, graves of whites surrounded the original Douglass section.

At lunchtime that first day at Washington School, Howell and Sam stood shivering off to one side of the playground and watched others play. As Howell recalled it years later, the next thing they knew, a "big-mouthed" local yelled "yellow britches, full of stitches." Not only were the England boys in new pants, but they were an uncommon yellow. Sam tore right into the heckler. He claimed his older brother had pushed him toward the taunting schoolmate with the charge to "take him." Truth is, Sam was not one to be trifled with. Howell's style was to negotiate, but he would never fail to back up his brother. The England boys stuck together.

Howell was a protective big brother. Back in Quitman, when young Sam was cutting some brush, his sharpened sickle struck him in the leg, causing blood to gush from the deep gash. Howell rushed to his side, ripped his pant leg, and used part of it to stem the flow, likely saving Sam's leg, if not his life

With the move to Maryville, Harvey and Hattie had their hands full. Their home was only a little more spacious than the one in Quitman, but it accommodated the six of them. There was enough land to develop a small truck farm, on which Harvey could raise produce to sell. Though her duties changed little, if any, Hattie had to orient herself to new surroundings, and her forty-nine-year-old husband had to find work to supplement his farm income. In addition to farming and ricking wood for sale, Harvey obtained a part-time job constructing cement walks and foundations in town. He also milked his cow Rose and raised some chickens and pigs. After butchering the fattened hogs (the Poland China was a favorite in Nodaway County), he rendered the lard. In time it became an additional source of income.

Before long the Englands had developed a routine. When work was slow, Harvey (almost invariably in a high-crowned hat)

walked to the square in the center of town. There he got acquainted with some of the local farmers and businessmen and reacquainted with his Quitman friends who came into town to sell produce. In good weather, loungers on the benches outside the courthouse casually discussed the day's activities. Some recalled the early mornings when heavy oxen-pulled wagons creaked and lumbered into town on their muddy wheels. Now, with better roads and automobiles, farmers could do their trading in the afternoon and be back home long before supper. Where teams of horses or oxen once swatted flies with their tails, autos carefully navigated the streets surrounding the square. They were intent on avoiding the cement-filled barrels on the four corners ordering them to "Go Slowly" and "Keep to the Right." Pedestrians were warned by painted, homemade signs proclaiming "No Jay Walking Allowed." This was a far cry from Quitman.

Saturday nights were special—stores were open late and drew crowds to town. Farm families came to sell produce, pick up their mail and newspapers (a week old), do their weekly shopping, and talk to old friends and acquaintances. In the summer, the square would be filled with families or small groups talking and laughing. Band concerts conducted under the electric streetlights were an occasional treat. When lit, the five globes resting atop fluted columns made it seem almost like day.

Everything seemed to revolve around the square, which held the courthouse at its center. Stores serving the town's needs surrounded the stately building. On the north side, for example, was the post office, Warren Jones's drug store, a barber shop (25¢ for a haircut, 15¢ for a shave, even a bath for another 15¢), and the Maryville Drug Company. In fact, at one time there were seven drug stores in town. On the west side was the Hudson Hardware Company, Derr Dry Goods Company (handling only piece goods), Sturm and Hagen Clothiers, Howndobler Drug Store, Elihu Jones's grocery, and the Nodaway Valley Bank.

The Empire and Electric theaters, particular enticements for the younger set, were just off the square. Pianists created a mood to match the action on the movie screens, which introduced a new world to Maryvillians. Mary Pickford, Theda Bara, and Pearl White entertained the men; in *Shoulder Arms*, Charlie

Chaplin brought his brand of comedy; and the dashing Douglas Fairbanks delighted the ladies in *The Knickerbocker Buckaroo.*

There were also plenty of churches, with three proclaiming themselves the "First" (the Baptist, Presbyterian and Christian), two Methodist Episcopal (one labeled "South"), two Roman Catholic (St. Mary's, the older, serving German Catholics, and St. Gregory's, which claimed Maryville's Irish and English Catholics), and two serving the African American community. However, the Englands did not attend with any regularity. They weren't non-believers; simply non-attenders.

Howell and Sam increasingly explored their new surroundings, looking for the best places to hunt and fish, usually on the 102 River. They were also drawn to the once-popular racetrack south of town. Overgrown with weeds, it was now barely visible. The surviving buildings, paddocks, and stables, which had formerly housed fine thoroughbreds, leaned precariously. It was fun for the boys to imagine what it must have been like when racing was at its peak, though they knew that their parents would never have allowed them to frequent such a place.

Nor did their parents want them hanging around the pool hall uptown, with its shady characters lounging behind the faded, drawn, once-blue blinds. Still, the unmistakable sounds of the clicking of pool balls and the shaking of dice behind that door created a tantalizing allure to the impressionable England brothers and their peers. Two years later, it became even more of a curiosity when the Eighteenth Amendment prohibited the sale of "intoxicating liquors."

The brothers often heard about and wished for the excitement of earlier times. In 1884, showman P.T. Barnum brought his "Greatest Show on Earth" to town, including "Jumbo." The famous elephant had already seized the attention of Londoners, and its name would come to describe anything very large. Barnum's circus train was ushered in on the Burlington line and his crew pitched tents on East Third Street, just north of the square.

Then there was an incident that would long be a subject of conversation. The Ringling Brothers, successors to Barnum, brought their big circus to town on September 18, 1905. Upwards of five thousand people gathered under the mammoth center tent erected on East First Street across from the Fair Grounds. Maryville, with a population of just four thousand, had drawn more circus attendees than St. Louis, the state's largest city. Not even the intermittent rain, which eventually became a downpour, scared away the assembled crowd awaiting the circus's midday opening. But around 3:00 p.m., well into the performance, a loud clap of thunder signaled an even greater storm. Almost half of the crowd took their leave. Less fortunate were the "Thousands of People Imprisoned within [the Tent's] Folds!" according to *The Nodaway Democrat's* headlines. A hurricane-force wind caused the "jumbo" tent to collapse and bury those who had remained under the water-soaked folds. In its inimitable style, the paper concluded that the "Scene Beggars Description!"

Lawsuits against the circus followed, but a federal court judge threw out the cases. The judge's decision was based in part on the testimony of a curious character known as "Aunt Betsy" Robinson, a former circus cook whom even the circus's lawyer labeled "bizarre." She wore pre-Civil War clothes, cussed, smoked, spit, often walked a sheep on a long rope, and "knew everything and everyone." In fact, the defendants' lawyer claimed that "Aunt Betsy" aided their case by distinguishing the liars from the truth tellers.

Yes, Maryville would prove an interesting place to its new residents, the Englands.

Nine-year-old Ruth was much less interested in circus stories or the crumbling vestiges of a racetrack. She had discovered the Carnegie Free Library, near the First National Bank, and shelves of books that she had not realized even existed. While she might scan the magazines or study the weather chart with its curious isothermal lines, it was what lay inside the covers of the books that attracted her. She would faithfully check out those books—one of which was *The Five Little Peppers and How They Grew*—return home, and by the dim light of an oil lamp, read to her heart's content. Poor Ruth had to endure years of being called "Polly Pepper" by her siblings. However, she introduced her sister to reading, and Rachie soon developed the same lifelong interest in the written word.

Before long, however, Americans' routines were interrupted by two major events: the Great War raging in Europe and the flu contagion of 1918. However, the Englands were fortunate—their lives were barely touched. The notorious Influenza of 1918—called the "Spanish Flu"—began innocuously enough: coughing and dizziness. This led to a backstabbing pain, and for many, death—twenty million worldwide and over half a million in the U.S., including ninety-four in Maryville. It wasn't the virus itself, but its side-effects (pneumonia mostly) that were fatal. Necessarily, schools were closed.

The first official notice was the quarantine sign placed on or near the front door of the sick person's or family's house. It meant only that the doctor or family could visit the patient. Semi-protected by gauze over the nose and mouth, caregivers (mostly family members) laboriously changed and washed germ-laden sheets and nightgowns.

While the Great War raged for almost four years, the Englands were safely away from the horrendous battles and appalling slaughter of Europe's youth. What began as an inexplicable assassination in an unpronounceable country had become a world war. Before it was over, five million Americans donned uniform and two million of them found themselves in Europe. In addition to volunteers and draftees, Maryville supplied its Battery C, 128th National Guard unit. Fortunately for the Englands, Howell and Sam were too young, and Harvey too old, to serve.

Among the draftees were three black men from Maryville: Ned Holmes, Arthur Smith, and Adolphus Gunn, grandson of Violet Gunn and uncle of Raymond Gunn. While just two years earlier, sixty white and African American veterans had sat together on Decoration Day (today Memorial Day), these three draftees were segregated for training and duty. It is unclear whether Douglass School teacher Ernest Boone Jr. served in a segregated unit. However, he did take officers training at Camp Pike, Arkansas, after enlisting in April 1918.

Then, on November 11, 1918, the war, touted as the one to "Make the World Safe for Democracy," was over. In only fifteen months, 116,516 Americans had died and the British and French lost roughly a million men each.

That first Armistice Day (later called Veterans Day) had special meaning for celebrants in Maryville. Two Civil War buglers—Nathaniel Sisson (wearing blue) and H.P. Childress (wearing Confederate gray)—marched at the head of the parade. Their playing of "Taps" at the courthouse brought tears to the eyes of many parade attendees.

In May 1919, Harvey went into business for himself and opened an ice plant. Harve—as he was now being called—saw an opportunity. For the most part, ice was available only in grocery stores and butcher shops. He would not only serve these establishments, but would also deliver ice to residents who had iceboxes. He explained to a *Democrat* reporter that he would handle only manufactured ice, which would be shipped from a plant in Burlington Junction. Having it shipped would take care of a number of problems. First, he wouldn't have to dig a large pond, from which he would have to cut the blocks in the winter. Second, he wouldn't have to build a large icehouse to store the fifteen to twenty tons of ice needed to last through the summer. But it didn't work out, and he never revealed why.

The year 1919 was a difficult one for the Englands; in fact, it was difficult for the whole country. Record rainfalls in September (over four inches in two days) flooded Maryville's pumping station on the 102 River, forcing it to close temporarily. Then it was record cold (nine below zero on December 9), made all the worse by the bituminous coal miners' (United Mine Workers) strike, which had begun in November and led to severe shortages. Business hours were curtailed; schools, churches, and even the CB&Q Railroad were shut down. To meet heating needs, teams of up to fifteen men were recruited to cut timber throughout the county. Many residents warmed themselves—and enjoyed some reading—at the Carnegie Library.

Prices rose as well. The price of eggs more than doubled, from 32¢ to 65¢ a dozen. Some of the inflation was blamed on the coal miners, who along with other unions, were threatening or initiating strikes. The Communists, who were bringing sweeping changes to Russia after the successful revolution in 1917, were accused of fomenting the labor problems. This "Red Scare" prompted Attorney General Mitchell Palmer to conduct raids on those he charged with being Communists. He also targeted the International Workers of the World (the "Wobblies"), which led to more strife.

President Woodrow Wilson's health had also become a major concern, although reports were rather vague. In September, his nation-wide trip to draw support for the Versailles Treaty and the League of Nations had ended abruptly with his debilitating stroke and hospitalization. His initial failure to respond to treatment brought the expected sympathy of many, but not support for his pet projects.

Racial tension was another postwar source of anxiety. In early October that year, James Malcolm, an African American shoe shiner at the Godsey Barber Shop on the north side of the square, reported being terrified by a lynching and courthouse burning during his visit to Omaha, Nebraska. On his return home, Malcolm exclaimed, "Maryville looks mighty good to me."

A white mob had lynched and burned Willie Brown, a black man accused of raping a white woman in Omaha. Brown's death was blamed in part on a race riot that began in the stockyards. It took greater than a thousand federal troops to restore order.

James Malcom was not the only one who praised race relations in Maryville. Years later, an African American woman from Maryville told a reporter she felt the same: "During the years, 1918 to 1935, that I lived in East Maryville, I never heard any bigoted talk against negroes." However, such Maryville experiences were not universal.

In 1898, the Rev. William M. Johnson, African American pastor of the Mt. Zion Baptist Church, denounced racism. In a previous church in Leavenworth, Kansas, he had urged parishioners to rise up against lynching, even if it meant dying. His outspokenness garnered him a great deal of public attention, and some suspect his sentiments may have led to the accusation that he made an indecent proposal to a white woman. After a warrant was issued, Johnson reported to the prosecutor, but fearing for his life, armed himself with two pistols. Intriguingly, he was allowed to hold onto one. On the day of the trial, a large crowd gathered in Maryville. A fearful Johnson, professing that "I will die before I will go down there and be lynched," asked to be taken to a safe place. The officers guarding him refused. Regrettably, discovering that Johnson still had one pistol in his jacket, an officer panicked and shot him, killing him instantly. The *Democrat Forum* tended to blame Johnson. He might have feared a lynching, but "nothing of that kind would have occurred" in Maryville.

However, that was long ago, and the incident had likely faded from the public memory. As he would throughout his life, Harve paid more attention to major league baseball and the 1919 World Series. He was pleased that the National Leaguers, the Cincinnati Reds, had beaten the Chicago White Sox five games to three. But he had heard some strange stories about how and why the Sox had lost. One story had it that some of the Sox players, hereafter called the "Black Sox," had thrown games for money. A year and a half later, Harve was pleased when commissioner Landis landed hard on those accused and barred eight from ever playing again. The integrity of baseball would be preserved. Harve prided himself on his honesty—his word was always good and he expected the same from others.

That honesty may have paid off, for Harve was elected president and superintendent of the Northwest Missouri Poultry Association. Despite the cold and the fuel shortage, he managed to conduct the association's nineteenth annual exhibition on December 8–11, 1919, in the empty Zook building on North Main Street. He assured officials of the Maryville Electric Light and Power Company and the Maryville Fuel Committee that he would not violate the fuel restrictions due to the miners' strikes and lived up to his word. Exhibitors came from as far away as Fort Morgan, Colorado. The exhibition was reported as a success, and no doubt was a factor in his re-election as president and superintendent for 1920.

Unfortunately, because of "the disturbed and unsettled condition of the country"—the continuing miners' strikes—the 1920 annual poultry exhibition was cancelled. Wanting to assure a successful 1921 exhibition, President Harve talked up the association at the annual meeting the following February. He encouraged the poultry association members to become more active: "Other associations are doing big things; let us keep abreast of changes." One change he suggested was to organize a boys' and girls' poultry club. The children would choose a breed to raise, be given eggs by association members and exhibit three chickens of the same breed at the December 1921 poultry show, which Harvey would again superintend. He offered two settings of his prized Buff Orpingtons to interested children, who eventually numbered close to one hundred and taxed the resources of the poultry association members. One of those children was his daughter Rachel, though she participated a bit reluctantly.

Despite her reluctance, Rachel entered the twentieth annual exhibition, held December 1–3, 1921, at the Martin building on the corner of First and Main streets. She took second place for the three Single Comb White Leghorns she raised. Harve also showed three Capons and seventeen Barred Plymouths. Once again, the show was considered highly successful. According to Superintendent England's report in the paper, there were almost seven hundred entries. The event was considered important enough that the Chamber of Commerce took moving pictures— still pretty much a novelty—of some of the prize-winning birds.

Harve also exhibited some of his prize chickens at the annual week-long County Fair, which had been held in Maryville since 1871. The biggest "Gala Week" in memory was the one held the year before, in 1920, which featured a band concert to open the fair. It was followed by the soldiers' and sailors' reunion the next day, the two-day pig show, and the usual showings of produce, canned goods, and other animals.

This year, streets around the square were roped off, and booths were set up. Lemonade stands, cotton candy stalls, and ice cream counters replaced the vehicular traffic. Homemakers proudly displayed their jellies, cakes, preserves, and canned goods. Farther away—though not far enough for some—was the long, smelly tarpaper building where various prize fowl, including guinea hens and pigeons, were proudly displayed by their owners. Still farther were the four-legged prizes: cattle, hogs, sheep, calves, brood mares, colts, stallions, and mules.

For many, the real excitement was generated by the side shows, featuring snake eaters, sword swallowers, oversized or undersized men and women, tattooed men, and a character who stuck safety pins, hat pins—really almost any pointed object that he could lay his hands on—into his bare upper body.

Everyone looked forward to Saturday night, the last night of the fair, when the four streets surrounding the courthouse teemed with festive fairgoers. Attendees threw confetti and rings at cane racks for prizes (that the winners probably didn't want the next day), whirled noise-making devices, and listened to the band, which competed with the calliope. Another drawing card was a bean-guessing contest. The electric light and power company was giving away an electric Maytag washer—which was displayed in one of its windows—to the individual who could guess the total number of red kidney beans. The very sight of the electric model and its automatic wringer, which was slowly replacing the noisy two-stroke, gas-powered engine, must have made some housewives drool.

If they desired other entertainment, moviegoers could pay their 22¢ (11¢ for children) to watch Douglas Fairbanks, Dorothy Gish, Billie Burke, or Theda Bara at the Empire or Electric, which changed shows daily.

Uptown for the fair, Hattie—recalling her experience at sister-in-law Rachel's millinery shop—examined the latest fashions. She couldn't help thinking about the changing shape of women's dresses. Critics felt that too many women had immodestly shortened their skirts and condemned the abandonment of corsets. Attempting to turn back the clock, a Utah bill aimed to bar women from wearing dresses higher than three inches above the ankle. The Virginia legislature tried to mandate similar restrictions.

Cosmetics ("the intoxication of rouge"), short hair, smoking, and drinking were other concerns of those preoccupied with female decency. Novelist F. Scott Fitzgerald captured the times when he revealed that a new indoor sport was "petting parties."

The increasing appearance of motorcars explains some of the cultural changes. So does the war. When young men went off to war, possibly not to return, many seized the moment, or at least became much more aware of their mortality. The war also had led to greater opportunities for women, as many had entered the workforce to replace men serving in the army. The achievement of suffrage in 1920 further bolstered the independence of women. Small town girls, including those in Maryville, were drawn to larger cities. Former old maids were going out on their own and renting kitchenette apartments. Women were attending college in greater numbers, and setting their sights on formerly male-dominated professions. Accompanying this growing independence was an empowering sense of agency, as divorce rates doubled between 1910 and 1928 and women led a franker life style.

Hattie could see some of this new independence in her young daughters.

Harve as fisherman, unknown date

But the England men retained some age-old customs, including celebrating the opening of the fishing season. Annually, on April 1, Harve and the boys would grab their licenses and head for the 102 River. Howell and Sam, with their wooden poles extending out over the river, mimicked their father in every aspect but one. Like a statue, he would remain immobile until the fish bit, which was unusually often. Howell tried his best, but he liked to talk. Sam could do a fair imitation of his father, though he too preferred more action. As much as they enjoyed fishing, the time spent together was more important.

Then there was the time when Sam made "Dad eat crow." The three of them were fishing, and Sam, who had an ample supply of a product called "Dan Sanders bait," offered some to his father. Harve just frowned—no one used artificial bait when worms, grasshoppers, and the like were on hand. Sam recalled that his father retorted, "Do you think fish are crazy?"

Their hooks were barely in the water when Sam yanked out a nice channel cat. Harve eyed him suspiciously. Another cat on Sam's line. Harve hadn't a bite. Yet another big channel, maybe a mud cat, grabbed Sam's line. Reluctantly acknowledging that the fish might be crazy, Harve turned to Sam and said, "Let's have some of your famous bait."

Another time, the "joke" was on Sam. After one fishing trip, Sam put a can of Dan Sanders bait above the door in the basement and promptly forgot about it. Before long, there was a terrible stench. He, Howell, and Harve all tried to locate the source, rearranging the entire basement to no avail. Then one day, Sam belatedly recalled where he had left it. The bait went out and the odor quickly disappeared, though a sheepish Sam never divulged the secret of the vanished odor.

Life was generally good for the Englands. They called Maryville "home." Between part-time jobs and his small farm, Harve was providing for his family. His leadership roles in the community also meant that he was becoming well known in the county. The children were doing well in school, and their future seemed promising. And Hattie, as she always would, quietly assured them a healthy home.

Chapter Four

The Englands Make Their Mark

Barely three years after he arrived in Maryville, Harve took on yet another responsibility. On December 1, 1921, while still busy with the exhibition, the Maryville merchants appointed him night watchman. Seemingly minor, this event would change the Englands' lives forever.

His unusual appointment resulted from an increase in robberies attributed to greater unemployment and train holdups. Police Chief E.E. Tilton had asked the city council to add a night watchman. The council demurred, but the merchants agreed to fund the additional protection. Harve's duty was to make regular nighttime trips around the business blocks and check doors to see that they were locked.

The fifty-three-year-old night watchman made his first arrest the very night of his appointment. After a trainman alerted him, Harve nabbed a vagrant who had tried to board a Wabash train without a ticket. The twenty-one-year-old from Rockford, Illinois confessed to having been a tramp for some time.

Four days later, Harve's exploits gained a measure of fame and earned a column in the paper, the first of many over the years. At 4:30 a.m., while making his rounds, he spotted a fire in the Gray Brothers' restaurant near a window facing the alley. Noticing sparks falling onto and burning a hole in the floor, he entered the building and dowsed the fire with buckets of water. Then he discovered open windows in the kitchen and the unlocked back door. The Grays praised England for saving their restaurant and the adjoining building. But nothing could be done about the theft, which the fire was set to cover up.

A month later, the new night watchman helped Mayor Fred Robinson and two city policemen arrest a pair of out-of-town moonshiners, who were arraigned the next day. While building a reputation as a lawman he was supplementing his income from farming and occasionally buying hogs for the Poland China (Hog) Association.

The England children were equally busy. Three of the children were now attending Washington School, and Howell was a member of the high school class of 1922. Sam was still a half grade behind, and Ruth four behind him. Rachie remained at the Garfield School for another year. Despite the daily chores they had to perform, the four children were becoming active members of the community. Howell, the first born, would continue to be the pathfinder—his engagement in athletics set an example for his siblings. However, Rachel did so reluctantly, preferring more sedate activities like reading.

It is a bit of a miracle that Howell was able to play at all, having sustained an injury in an accident back in Quitman. Howell's Sunday School teacher was driving his pupils home, and because the buggy was over-crowded, Howell was hanging out. The horse ran into a pole and Howell's foot was crushed, leaving him with a slight limp the rest of his life.

Nevertheless, in 1920, he and Sam, both high school juniors, made the football team—though neither was first team. Described in the school paper as "gritty" and "smart," Howell earned his athletic letter, the small green "M" with a white outline. However, as would always be the case, Sam garnered more notice. He was a guard, and while "too light" to make the first team, Sam was reported to be a "good fighter." Both boys could claim some credit, as they were members of the Maryville football team that lost only one game. They outscored their opponents 241–35 and won three games by the total of 153–0! Sam tried to stifle his emotion when awarded his full-sized "M" at the awards banquet in February 1921. The event's significance was underscored by the bigwigs who spoke: the college president, chamber of commerce president, high school superintendent, and the college football coach.

The next year, their senior year, both played more, but again Sam took the honors by playing on the first team. While the "yellow britches" boys attended the awards banquet again, they were already focusing their attention on making the basketball team. Competition was strong, with sixty boys trying out. Ten teams of six went head-to-head for the ten-man limit. Sam captained tryout Team VIII, which won its first two games, while Howell's Team III was eliminated in the first round. Sam made the regular team, but mostly he was rewarded by splinters. Nonetheless, he was a member of the team that won the Northwest Missouri High School Association title in March.

Meanwhile, Howell took the stage and played Jennings the butler in the high school play, "My Friend From India." The next night, January 20, 1922, he graduated with fourteen classmates. Four days later, his younger sister Ruth and twenty-four classmates were promoted to the high school.

Before Sam would graduate in May, he would lead the combined senior-freshman classes against the sophomore-junior boys in the annual class "fight" on the school football field. The object, in addition to blowing off steam at the end of the school year, was to grapple in the dust and tie with ropes every member of the opposing team. At 10:00 p.m. the two teams collided. Before long, Sam's freshman teammates were overcome by their opponents and called for help. But Sam's senior teammates were outnumbered. For an hour the seniors put up a good fight, but it was not enough. Then the final ignominy—bound, the losers were thrust into waiting cars and taken anywhere from one to ten miles out of town, where they were dropped off. Of course, as the team captain, Sam was rewarded by one of the longer rides.

Then, like his older brother, he too was a graduate of Maryville Senior High School.

Initially, the 1920s portended a good time for Harve and other farmers. The war demands had led many farmers to expand their operations. But Harve knew his limits—he had enough land for his purposes and limited equipment. On his small truck farm, he raised for-market chickens, a variety of fruits (mostly strawberries and raspberries), potatoes, and corn. He even had letterheads printed:

HARVE ENGLAND

FRUITS AND VEGETABLES

ROUTE 4

MARYVILLE, MO

He was quite proud of the results of his efforts, and periodically honored the editor of the *Daily Democrat-Forum* with a box of strawberries. It paid off when the editor noted that on May 27, 1922, "Mr. England" expected to pick almost five thousand boxes of strawberries. However, Harve left nothing to chance, and himself advertised "The Famous Senator Dunlap" strawberries available either at the grocers or at his patch.

Harve loved his berries, even later when—irritatingly—the seeds would get under his dentures. Early morning in season, he picked the berries and tenderly put them in small pint and quart baskets for sale while retaining some for the family. Back in the house, he poured milk on and lightly sugared a dishful of the berries. His common out-of-season dessert was buttered bread on which he also sprinkled sugar. Despite sugaring his desserts, Harve remained lean.

Second only to his taste for berries was his liking for biscuits. Writing to Hattie from St. Joe two years earlier, he closed his letter by asking her to "have some biscuits and bacon for [him]" when he arrived home the next day. Harve was hungry and tired after buying and loading hogs at the stockyards in St. Joseph, Maryville's larger neighbor to the south. Along with the biscuits, he wanted Hattie to call "the boys," other members of the Poland China Association, to meet him at the depot to unload his purchases.

On January 9, 1922, Hattie's father Byron, reputed to be one of the county's oldest citizens, died at age eighty-two. Hattie accepted the news with mixed feelings. She was now free from his control. The tie was finally broken, except for her father's law books, which were still in her care. Still, she recognized that—however crusty and domineering—he was her flesh and blood. The next day, she and Harve drove over to the Ohio cemetery in

Burlington Junction and laid Byron to rest. And she would get on with her life.

As always, Hattie was interested in local and world news. Unfortunately, the news was often gloomy. The Bolsheviks were forcefully establishing power in Russia. Germany's finances had collapsed, and the French government seemed on the verge of a collapse, though it had invaded the Ruhr. The Fascisti had gained control of Italy, and the United States had refused to join the League of Nations.

The domestic scene was little brighter. During a month of official mourning for President Harding, "Silent Cal" Coolidge had been sworn in. He and the nation would have to deal with the scandals of the Harding administration, of which, as vice president, he had been a member. Race riots, workers' strikes, and lynchings by the Ku Klux Klan also occupied the news.

News about the KKK particularly disturbed Hattie, as the organization had fairly recently shown its ugly face in the Midwest. Founded in Tennessee in 1866, it had spread to almost every Southern state by 1870. It violently attacked the Republican Party's Reconstruction policies, which were intended to provide equality, while simultaneously promoting white supremacy. After a decline in the early twentieth century, it was revived around 1915 by white nativists, inspired in part by Thomas Dixon's book *The Clansman* and D.W. Griffith's movie *Birth of a Nation*. Within five years, membership numbered four million.

The condition of the economy also was troubling. Nineteen state banks had closed, gasoline prices had seesawed from a high of 22.8¢ to a low of 11¢ per gallon, and Maryville's weather had been just as volatile and troubling. Unpredictable and changeable weather disturbed regular growth and harvest cycles. Too much rain drowned plants; too little, of course, starved them. Animals dependent on grass or hay consequently were affected.

In the fall of 1922, Howell broke new ground when he became the first in his family on either side to attend college, let alone high school. Up on the northwest side of town, Northwest Missouri State Teachers College, only fifteen years old, represented Maryville's stake in the future. Establishing it had not been easy for the town.

Seventy years earlier, following the lead of Massachusetts and neighboring Iowa, Missouri had created a school for training teachers in St. Louis. In short order, normal schools were created in northeast, central, and southeast Missouri. Only the northwestern part of the state was unrepresented. Beginning in 1873, Nodaway County residents sought a similar school to serve their part of the state. They decided it ought to be in Maryville, the county seat, and in 1880 the Maryville Normal School (more accurately an institute) opened and ran summer sessions for about fourteen years. It was briefly succeeded by another institute formed by a group of businessmen. The new school, called the Maryville Seminary, operated for a time under the control of Maryville's Methodist Church.

Nevertheless, belief in the need for a state-certified normal school did not die, and money was pledged for a school beginning in 1894. Seven years later, emboldened western Missouri representatives approached the state legislature with a new proposal. Though the legislature turned them down, their hopes remained alive. In 1905, they desperately countered a last-minute bid by Savannah to locate the normal school in adjoining Andrew County. Nodaway County was successful, though not without a flurry of visits by state officials. Two years later, over the opposition of a newly formed group from Andrew County, the Northwest Missouri Normal School began operations. The Maryville High School (for summer sessions), the old Seminary, and the Methodist church (for daily chapel) were readied for the opening convocation on June 13, 1906, with 212 students enrolled. A year later, the cornerstone for the new building was laid.

Objections continued to be raised and overcome, and finally, on October 3, 1910, students attended classes in the new building.

By 1922, when Howell entered, the school bore the more academic name Northwest Missouri State Teachers College (NWMSTC). Despite his less than spectacular success in French, Howell did all right at the college, and like most of the students, was headed toward a teaching career. Despite his limp, he managed to play football and receive the coveted "M" letter his last two years. On January 29, 1923, his sister Ruth's fifteenth birthday, he seemed particularly out of character. Dressed in overalls and carrying a hatchet, he left his family open-mouthed. He even attended classes that way and had his picture taken with eleven others. That night, a proud Howell England was inducted into the "M" Club. Although outwardly calm, even shy, he was aflutter. Old "yellow britches" had proven himself.

Similarly, Harve was beginning to make his mark in the community. On May 1, 1923, at the relatively advanced age of fifty-five and only six years after arriving in Maryville, Harve, a Democrat, was appointed chief of police by the newly-elected Republican mayor W.O. Garrett. A month later, as the *Democrat-Forum* reported, Harve donned an "official, navy blue uniform, trimmed with brass buttons and white stripes" and became a "custodian of municipal peace and tranquility." Typical of small-town America, his duties were quite commonplace, mostly apprehending drunks and disturbers of the peace. He dutifully enforced the new parking ordinance requiring curb parking rather than the previous practice of parking in the center of the street. "You gain from two to three times as much parking space by side parking," he told the reporter for the paper, "which has been tried and found successful in large cities." Further, he implemented the city's plan to paint safety zones for pedestrians at street corners, a measure intended to eliminate jay walking.

That Halloween, he hired three extra watchmen to quell pranks and mischief. In the following week's paper he praised the community for the relative quiet, studiously ignoring an incident involving the old Indian statue. The statue, normally outside the cigar store, had been snatched and put in place of the life-size statue of Hebe, the Greek goddess of youth, in the college administration building. In fact, with the exception of an undisclosed but minor threat by the KKK, the year was a particularly quiet one for him, with less than a third of the arrests from the previous year and less than a fifth of those in 1921.

Though he may have harbored ambition, Harve appeared content. His pay was not munificent, but it was steady. Between that and his farm income, the family would be all right. They were healthy and active, and the four younger ones were achieving a degree of independence. Howell and Sam, both now at the college, derived some income from enlisting and serving in Battery C, 128th Missouri National Guard, an artillery unit. As quartermaster sergeant, Howell worked and roomed in the armory. While there was no indication Howell resented it, Sam was elected lieutenant and outranked his older brother. Ironically, they would both outrank their father, who enlisted in February 1924 as a private and enjoyed some additional income.

Such an arrangement was common, as the Guard's small permanent staff was augmented by male college students. Though they drilled weekly and trained at Fort Riley, Kansas, two weeks each summer, they were anything but combat ready. They were probably better known for marching in parades in their starched khaki uniforms studded with shiny brass.

Perhaps an indicator that Harve was not quite as content as he appeared, a month short of a year as police chief, he resigned—ostensibly to devote more time to his small farm. But the scuttlebutt was that he intended to run for sheriff. The *Democrat-Forum* correctly predicted that he would use the time to "do a little campaigning" before the August primaries. In fact, Harve was already campaigning. He was reported to have boasted that every arrest he had made during the past eleven months had resulted in a conviction. He also stressed that in making those arrests, he "never had occasion to use his .45 for bringing down a fugitive."

It's unclear when he told Hattie—who no doubt anticipated it—of his plans. She worried that the responsibilities of the sheriff were too heavy a burden. To complicate things, he had only driven a horse-drawn wagon since his sister's death four decades earlier, and reluctantly at that. How did he expect to get out on calls?

But Harve had thought through such obstacles. He was tired of arresting drunks and chasing stray dogs, and craved the greater responsibilities of the sheriff. If needed, his deputies could drive. His term as chief was only for a year, so there was a chance that he could be out of job soon anyway. The family needed a source of steady income, and farming was always too problematic to make a steady living.

In fact, that year colder-than-normal temperatures lasted well into summer, and heavy spring and summer rains flooded crops, reducing the corn output to 64 percent of normal. To top it off, "crown borers" destroyed the roots of some of the plants. Like other farmers, Harve had to plow under the affected plants and replant what he could in a new patch. But Harve didn't have the luxury of additional acreage. Even with the extra income from the Guards, it would be tough going.

And so, on April 1, Harve filed his candidacy on the Democratic ticket. His friends had told him that filing early was the secret. Sure enough, just seven days later, Lowell B. Campbell, a furniture dealer, undertaker, and third-term mayor of nearby Barnard, filed his candidacy on the Democratic ticket. The entry of Campbell, the son of a county court judge and member of his town's Democratic party, would deliver Harve a powerful opponent.

When another Maryvillian, Harvey Walter, filed his candidacy, Harve found himself in a race against Campbell, Walter, and the GOP's four candidates. To the extent that $33 would help the cause, Harve was an active campaigner. In addition to the $5 filing fee, newspaper ads cost Harve $15, campaign cards used up another $8, hiring a car used up $2, and following custom, he purchased $3 worth of cigars to pass out. As a non-smoker, that was more than enough for his tastes.

Due to his reluctance to engage in what he considered distasteful campaigning, Harve was outspent almost seven to one by Campbell. Despite this inequity, Harve picked up 750 votes to Campbell's 1,027. In fact, Harve outpolled all the candidates but Campbell, the eventual winner, in the general election. Moreover, because of the one-term limit, Harve was in a good position to make a successful run for sheriff in four years.

With the race over, Harve gave his full attention to his farm. One morning, he and fourteen pickers harvested more than 640 quarts of strawberries in just over four hours. He then turned to cultivating his other berry and grape plots. Typically, the editor of the local paper duly reported Harve's activities.

His prize chickens, which supplied the eggs that daughters Ruth, sixteen, and Rachie, fourteen, delivered for him on the way to school, also occupied his attention. In early fall, Harve was once more re-elected Superintendent of the Northwest Missouri Poultry Association Annual Show and helped with the planning. It was a thankless job, but it offered a chance to compare notes with other poultry raisers. Perhaps more importantly, it allowed Harve to remain in the public eye, strange as it might seem for one so reticent. Poultry was big business; the county was reported to have 513,190 chickens in 1930 while the state average was 278,788.

Meanwhile, in early October Harve served as one of eleven "special police" for the three-day Farm and School Show. His duties included directing traffic and "keeping order," tasks with which he was more than a little familiar. He was glad for the opportunity to keep in practice and make some money.

Somehow, ignoring the unusually scorching heat, Harve found time to walk uptown to stand with others outside the *Democrat-Forum* office, to which the Hanamo Telephone Company supplied radio service. Harve could "experience" some baseball games while they were being played. Unfortunately, this year his favorite team, the St. Louis Cardinals, was not in the World Series. John McGraw's New York Giants had taken the pennant again, as they did too often. Harve, who could not pass up a game, still dropped in daily to catch the action on Omaha's WOW or one of the Chicago radio stations. Harve was fascinated by the dialing necessary to catch the right wavelength. WOW, for instance, was way up on the dial at 508.2 meters, along with WIP and WOO in Philadelphia.

Even if he missed a game, Harve would become captivated by the working of this electrical wonder. He had even heard rumors that Shenandoah, across the border in Iowa, was going to have a station. Henry Field, the nurseryman, wanted a way to enter homes to deliver his sales messages. Of course, if 'ol Henry did it, so too would Earl May, Field's major competitor just across the flats from him. Indeed, Field shortly had his radio station (KFNF) and May his KMA. Harve didn't care which of them was successful, for both major nurseries served him well. For years their broadcasts were a staple for many farmers.

At the same time, Harve followed his sons' activities, though he didn't understand their interest in football. An adaptation of English rugby, football had appeared in a few Eastern U.S. colleges in the second half of the nineteenth century. Due to serious injuries, growth slowed early in the twentieth century, but by this time high schools and colleges throughout the U.S. fielded teams.

Sam, a year behind Howell at the college, continued to upstage his brother in athletics. In fact, the 175-pounder would captain the undefeated 1925 Bearcat team on which Howell was a teammate. *The Tower*, the NWMSTC yearbook, asserted that "Sam, a tackle, had an uncanny faculty for breaking up line plays." With dark hair and eyes to match, the mustachioed Sam, "A bold, bad man!" according to *The Tower*, would win four letters to his brother's two. (Sixty years later Sam would become just the fifteenth member of the Northwest Missouri University "M" Club Hall of Fame.)

In late November 1924, Harve superintended the Annual Northwest Poultry Association show for the fifth straight year. Held above George McMurry's garage on Fourth and Market streets, the three-day show attracted entrants who brought more than five hundred birds. While he enjoyed seeing the birds, comparing notes, and attending to many details of the judging, Harve was growing tired of the responsibility.

Then, just before the year's end, Harve entered the annual turkey shoot, which he won with remarkable regularity. This time, Howell tried—unsuccessfully—to give him some competition.

The year 1925 opened quietly enough for Harve, but that would change. One January morning he ran into newly-installed Sheriff Lowell Campbell. The conversation went something like this, Harve later recalled: "Afternoon, Harve," Campbell said, "Unusually warm for January." Then, after a brief pause, "I need another deputy, someone familiar with Maryville and respected. As former police chief, you are a natural. What do you say?" Harve was not as surprised as Campbell had anticipated. There had been rumors that the sheriff might approach him. After a pause for effect, Harve agreed to serve and Campbell indicated he would make the appointment shortly. So, on January 20, 1925, Harve England was appointed a deputy.

Hattie reluctantly accepted his decision. There would be a steady income to supplement the farm, though she worried about Harve's well being. The girls could keep her company when not participating in school activities, with which they were increasingly involved.

Daughter Ruth, a class officer, was active in the high school historical society, for which she gave a couple of talks, and was in a school play. Like her older brothers, she too participated in athletics. The past year she had played intramural basketball, helping her class win a tournament. Better yet, she played guard on the high school's interscholastic basketball team. Possibly her biggest accomplishment was taking second place (out of 30 contestants) in the javelin throw in the county track meet.

Less interested in athletics, Rachel was involved in the science and history clubs and the Elizabethan Literary Society. Her older sister thought she might also have been drawn to these male-dominated organizations for other than academic reasons.

While the sisters generally got along well, Hattie occasionally had to intercede in disagreements. Often, this involved Rachel's "borrowing" of Ruth's clothes, which Ruth had bought with money derived from a variety of out-of-school jobs. In addition to delivering her father's eggs, she helped out at Dr. Ryan's office and picked strawberries and raspberries in season.

Meanwhile, Harve had barely pinned on his deputy's badge and holstered his .45 when he was sent out to find an escapee, one of three mercantile store robbers. The escapee had sawed his way out of the county jail and driven away in a stolen car. At 5:00 a.m. on February 2, Harve set out for Lincoln, Nebraska, with Sheriff Campbell's brother and another deputy. They were sent to retrieve the escapee and the other two robbers who had been apprehended by Cornhusker state policemen. Wanting to hold the escapees for crimes committed in their state, however, the Nebraska authorities refused to give up the prisoners. Frustrated, the deputies returned to Maryville with only the recovered loot. Two weeks later, Harve and the sheriff, who had "dickered" with his Nebraska counterparts to produce the prisoners, successfully returned with them.

Though busy, Harve found time for hunting, one of his favorite sports. One outing south of town resulted in his killing a twelve-pound rabbit. An impressed *Democrat-Forum* editor duly reported the unusual kill in the paper after Harve showed it to the courthouse hangers-on. However, the editor teased Harve about his claim to have spotted a robin on February 5 by quoting a skeptical fellow deputy: "I think [Harve] is about the biggest prevaricator in the county, on this occasion [early in the year]." However teasing, Harve's appearance in the press was always overwhelmingly positive.

As Hattie anticipated, Harve seemed to be out nightly, mostly scouring for the ubiquitous moonshiners. Well, scouring is not exactly correct, for operators of many of the stills were well known. The trick was to find the stills. For example, on February 3, Harve and Sheriff Campbell found an empty five-gallon jug and two one-gallon jugs in the manger of a barn! The owner of the farm claimed he didn't know anything about the liquor. The next day, Harve, Campbell, and police chief Bernard "Barney" Dougan found a still and four pints of corn whiskey at a house in the south part of town. The operator pled guilty, claiming that he made the whiskey to support his family. In mid-March, a bigger haul was made outside Burlington Junction when Harve, Deputy Rasco, and Sheriff Campbell discovered a copper boiler estimated to produce fifty gallons a day, four empty five-gallon jugs, two oil stoves, two barrels of rye mash (in a cave), two copper coils (under stumps in a ditch), 350 pounds of brown sugar, and a hundred-pound sack of sugar in the barn oat bin! A week later, Harve arrested a moonshiner who had hidden a gallon of liquor in a woodpile. Still another time, a blind thirty-five-year-old piano tuner was arrested for possession of a pint of corn whiskey. Though a teetotaler, Harve could sympathize with some of these miscreants who were simply trying to make a passable living off their wits.

Other forays resulted in arrests for offenses, which ran the gamut from forgery, robbery, and disturbing the peace to illegal crap games. The latter induced the *Democrat-Forum* editor to rib Harve in the paper. It seems the sheriff received a call (likely from a loser) that a game of "African dominoes" (black men shooting craps) was in progress in a cornfield south of the village of Ravenwood. As the editor reported the incident, "The sheriff and his deputy [Harve] made plans to surround the gang that was waxing 'hot.' As it happened, Sheriff Campbell ran into the bunch first," causing the participants to hightail it. The unfortunate Harve, the editor clucked, "was laboriously making his way through the dense forest of corn stalks, and to make the matters worse he had to wade through a small lake up to his knees in water to get to the road and worse yet, Harve missed all the fun of seeing the crap shooters scatter." Good-naturedly, Harve stopped by the editor's office to protest the treatment he had received in the paper.

Restoring his reputation, Harve helped prevent a jailbreak when he discovered that two bars on the outside of a jail window and part of one on the inside had been sawed through. The subsequent search by him, the sheriff, and Police Chief Dougan uncovered two saws, two case knives, and a file, as well as the culprit, though the mystery of how the tools got into the jail remained unsolved.

Though concerned about Harve's health, Hattie had to admit that her husband of a quarter century was holding up well. Maybe his physical activity helped him to remain healthy. Still, she knew that one of these nights a moonshiner might try to evade arrest by drawing a .12 gauge shotgun. Or the car in which Harve was riding might turn over on a slippery road or hit a stray hog. She wished he could make do on the farm alone or a combination of the farm and some safer part-time job. But she shared her thoughts only with her diary. Admittedly and all things considered, the year had been relatively quiet.

Then, bundling up against the subzero temperature, she watched the snowfall and listened to her clock tick away another year.

Chapter Five

The Transitional Years

The subzero temperatures that had ushered out 1925 lingered into January of 1926. Worse, the news, international, national, or local—it made little difference—would do nothing to warm the Englands in the upcoming months.

The *Democrat-Forum* editor, following the Missouri governor's lead, tried to remain optimistic, but it was difficult. The debate over the utility of Prohibition would heat up again, as would arrests of moonshiners. Bank closings would increase, including the county's second oldest bank. The trials of principals in the Teapot Dome scandal during the Harding administration would continue to embarrass the nation. Gang wars would spread from cities to the coalmines in southern Illinois. And mourning following the appendicitis-induced death of movie heartthrob Rudolph Valentino would occupy reams of newspaper near the end of August.

The world news was even more depressing. Over one hundred thousand uniformed German ex-soldiers would march in Nuremberg, suggesting a revival of the Fatherland. Coal prices would escalate, due to strikes in England and the U.S.

Yet, Hattie and Harve were comforted that they and their family were relatively healthy. Howell and Sam would graduate from NWMSTC later in the year—Sam in May and Howell in August.

With the growing season approaching, Harve took stock. In early March, he purchased lots 46, 47, and 48 in the South

Park division from Bob Rice and his wife. Harve paid $435 for the 145 by 214 foot tract (just over a half acre), which abutted his property near the southern city limits. Though it meant more work, he needed more land to raise enough crops to support his family. Hattie agreed to the purchase, glad that Harve would be focusing more on farming.

Despite the added labor of cultivating the extra land, Harve found time for his deputy duties. In fact, 1926 would result in even more raids on moonshiners and their stills. On just the fourth day of the new year, Harve was involved in two raids: one on the Star Barn on East Second Street, the other on East Fifth Street. Both, ironically, were within a few blocks of the sheriff's office at the jail. The first raid brought considerable satisfaction to the arresting officers. A barn is one of the hardest places to find illicit booze, and the operator was considered the biggest violator of the law in the county.

Harve as Maryville, Missouri police chief

One of Harve's more exciting raids occurred in early April. The suspect distracted Harve and the two other deputies by attempting to ride away on a horse while his wife raced to the house. Once inside, she quickly began smashing the evidence on the edge of a stone jar. By the time the arresting officers entered the house, the wife had broken four bottles, spilling the contents onto the kitchen floor. Unfortunately for her and her husband, she managed only to knock the top off the fifth bottle, leaving enough liquor for the authorities to take back to Maryville as evidence. Neither Harve nor the other two officers had ever attempted to arrest such a wild member of the opposite sex previously. Dutifully, they brought her in, only to have a judge release her because she had two small children.

Responding to the hazards of the job, Sheriff Campbell increased his "artillery" less than two weeks later. The sheriff introduced a double-barreled, foot-long, "sawed-off" shotgun, which he claimed was "feared by criminals." Word had it that the weapon was popular with Chicago policemen, bank guards, and security forces in other institutions countering crime. Possibly for effect, Campbell also reported to the paper that he, his deputies, and the police chief were practicing frequently and were "proficient" with it. If that were not enough, the sheriff reminded readers that he and his deputies still had their repeater riot guns. Harve was reputed to be the most proficient marksman with both guns. Yet, after seven years as a part-time lawman, he still had never felt it necessary to draw his .45 to make an arrest.

Neither the sawed-off shotgun nor the riot guns were necessary for the arrest of five farm youths out for a good time with a jug of liquor in their Ford car. Nor was any of that artillery needed to nab the dispenser of the liquor, whose whereabouts were revealed by the youths in exchange for a lighter sentence. Harve and the sheriff had barely landed back in town when they were called out to a dance near Wilcox. They were rewarded by two arrests and six pints of "red liquor." A short time later, Harve was embarrassed by the arrest of a distant cousin on a charge of felonious assault. Escorting two sheep thieves back from St. Joseph soon after proved a more pleasant experience.

As Harve suspected, the sheriff's mid-year report revealed an increase in crime—at least convictions—in the county. In just the eighteen months of Campbell's term, thirty-four persons had received penitentiary sentences and 268 had been incarcerated in the county jail. The number was greater than the entire previous four-year period and that pace would be maintained through the rest of the year. Sheriff Campbell attempted no explanation.

But it was not all work for Harve. To celebrate Sam's graduation from NWMSTC and Ruth's graduation from high school, the proud family gathered for a photograph. Though in the front row, as always, Hattie did her best to try to hide. Harve, whose short-cropped, stiff hair was only beginning to show gray, properly sported a bow tie for the occasion. Howell appeared as the proper would-be school administrator. The girls, both combing their hair to touch just above the eye, offered a symmetry. Rachie wore a stylish light-colored dress, aiming to stand out against the others' dark outfits. Characteristically, Ruth preferred a more subdued color. Sam, perhaps living up to his "bold, bad" image, glowered under his dark eyebrows. Strangely, none appeared particularly happy.

Sam would land a job teaching physical education and coaching the "Savages" at Savannah High School, down the road from Maryville. Howell would serve as principal and coach at Fortescue, over near the Missouri River. Both were close enough to come home often, especially if needed. Ruth would enter NWMSTC, studying U.S. History during the ten-week summer session. Rachel remained in high school two more years.

In mid-July, Harve briefly joined the excited crowd surrounding the water tower. Two Omaha smokestack workers had hauled themselves up the landmark water tower to apply a shiny new coat of black paint. Harve was equally intrigued when the Cook family opened the Missouri Theater, spending an astronomical $75,000. The owner was equipping the theater for "talkies," an innovation which Harve viewed skeptically.

England family photo ca. 1926. Sitting l to rt: Harriette, Ruth, Rachel, Harve. Standing: Samuel, J.H.

For some reason, Harve took no interest in the Dempsey-Tunney fight in September. Nor could he understand Hattie's interest. Stranger yet, until Howell took up the game in high school, she showed no interest in baseball, the national pastime. Yet, she knew challenger Gene Tunney was an ex-marine who read Shakespeare. And that he had licked former heavyweight champion Jack Dempsey, sharing in the nearly two million dollar gate!

For Harve, baseball was a true sport (next to hunting and fishing, of course). Though he had tried, he could not avoid catching a mild dose of the pennant fever that had gripped many Missourians in 1926. A St. Louis team hadn't won a league championship since 1888. Now his Cardinals had finally done it, though the race had been nip and tuck well into September. The trick was acquiring Grover Cleveland Alexander, now considered washed up, for $4,000. Just three years earlier, the Chicago Cubs had offered him to the Cardinals for an astronomical $100,000 ($1.3 million in 2015). Ironically, two days after the trade, "Old Pete" licked his former teammates 3–2 in ten innings.

Unwilling to spend seventy-five hard-earned dollars for a Crosley radio that looked more like a piece of furniture, on game days Harve found a spot near one of the radios at Holt's Supply Company on the north side of the square.

Miller Huggins's New York Yankees, the 6–5 favorites to win the Series, edged Harve's Cards 2–1 in the first game, behind the pitching of Herb Pennock. But the Cards got even two days later, when Old Pete, giving up only five hits and striking out ten, put the Yankees and Urban Shocker down 6–2. Harve was excited. Back home on Tuesday, October 5, the Cards did it again. Big Jess Haines not only didn't give up a run in the 4–0 victory, but also drove in two runs with a homer. Harve was sure this was the Cardinals' year. But, the next day, the Yankees' Babe Ruth homered three times to even the series. Then Pennock put the Yankees ahead in a 3–2, ten-inning game. Two days later Alexander, proving that he still had his stuff, won big, 10–2. The Yankees' big threats, Babe Ruth and Lou Gehrig, managed only one hit between them—Gehrig's single.

On Monday, October 11, in a crowd that stretched out the door of Holt's, the usually reserved deputy was surprisingly anxious. The World Series had come down to one game. He was sure this would be the Cardinals' game—and year.

The Cards' early score seemed to confirm his judgment, but the Babe tied the game in the third inning with a home run off Haines, setting a record for round trippers. The Cards recaptured the lead in the seventh, but their starter filled the bases.

Cupping his ear to catch the scratchy sound coming from the radio, Harve was astonished to hear the announcer report that Alexander was coming on in relief. Old Pete, washed up Pete, who had already pitched and won two games? With the Yankees' young shortstop Lazzeri at bat? A ball. Then a strike followed by another ball. Then another strike. Normally reserved Harve must have wiped some moisture from his lip, but relaxed momentarily when Alexander got out of that inning, fanned the Yankees in the eighth, and held on to win the game. The Cardinals and Old Pete were the World Series champions! After sharing the excitement with others for a short time, an exhausted, but pleased, Harve England started his long walk home.

Less than a week after the series concluded, Harve and Hattie were entertained—no, intrigued—by a football game. Despite virtual ignorance of the game, they obtained a ride to Savannah, some forty miles south, to see son Sam's football team play Maryville's. Just as it had when Howell and Sam played, it seemed to the parents that this game made no sense. Twenty-two boys, momentarily lined up in some semblance of order, then battered each other for possession of a funny-looking ball. At least their son, Coach England, was plainly visible on the sideline, exhorting his boys to greater effort. Unfortunately, Sam's charges were unsuccessful against his alma mater's team

Harve's interest in Sam's budding career drew the attention of the *Democrat-Forum* editor early the next year. "Harve England, deputy sheriff" was reported to have become "a rabid basketball fan." The editor claimed that Harve was "stirring around town inquiring about the results of the Benton High School of St. Joseph-Savannah boys game last night." Then, Harve was reported to look "rather downcast" after having discovered that his son's team had been beaten decisively, 36–18.

If there was any game about which Harve was "rabid," it was Cribbage. He often sought the opportunity to retrieve the wooden board, pegs, and cards, and challenge his friends. It relaxed him. He could spend hours bent over the Cribbage board. While talking was always at a minimum, he loved the company and competition.

Perhaps his interest in raising chickens and the competition for prize money explained why he had agreed to serve as superintendent of the poultry show for the past seven years. But 1926 was to be his last year. Harve had tired of setting up the exhibitions, although he still enjoyed the show itself. By mid-November, he had commitments from breeders from more than twenty-eight counties in Missouri, Iowa and Kansas. This year, the show would even feature some rare birds. He had to admit—even after so many years—that he took satisfaction from the first place prize awarded his Barred Plymouth Rock Cocks.

The fall of 1926 gave way to winter. With winter came rising coal prices, due more to strikes than increased demand. Harve and Hattie had become even more conscious of their modest income. As the *Democrat-Forum* had informed "Mrs. Housewife," Hattie found that Christmas dinner for her family would be more expensive than last year. According to the U.S. Department of Agriculture, for ten dollars a family of five could have a "turkey with chestnut stuffing and giblet gravy, mashed potatoes, Brussels sprouts, celery, cranberry sauce, tomato aspic salad, plum pudding and hard sauce, nuts, fruit and coffee." Chicken, candied sweet potatoes, cauliflower, cranberry sauce, grape fruit, nut salad, mince pie and coffee could be prepared for five dollars. A dinner for half that price would feature pork loin. Fortunately, the paper reported that almost six million pounds of turkey and in excess of eighty-four million barrels of apples were in storage for American shoppers.

Braving the unusual subzero cold, the Englands went uptown to do some shopping, at least "window shopping." Howell had driven home for the weekend and offered his parents a ride to the square. Though never stylish, even embarrassed by her looks, Hattie admired a smart sports dress in one store window. She closely examined the featured zipper. Missing were the familiar, but frustrating, dress hooks and snaps. In fact, zipper fastenings, once relegated only to tobacco pouches, were now showing up on galoshes, handbags, corsets, underwear, and gowns. Hattie was told that in larger cities, like Omaha and Kansas City, she could buy zipper fastenings by the yard. Zippers on children's clothes could be a lifesaver. Hattie dreamily recalled her days in Rachie Smith's millinery shop, but her reflection in the store window snapped her back to reality.

On the final day of the year, the *Democrat-Forum* blared, "deputy sheriff [Harve] an expert shot with rifle and shot gun," captained the "Bunny Busters" against Hayden Soners's "Bushwhackers." The object was to bring into town the greatest number of rabbits, which would be counted and then shipped to the "New York market." "Nothing in the way of arms [rifle, single shot, double barrel, or pump gun] was prohibited," the paper reminded readers. While Harve didn't win the silver medal for bagging the most rabbits, his was the winning team. More importantly, the money from selling the rabbits to the local produce dealer went to support the Maryville Welfare Board. The board found itself in greater need this year than usual.

The new year—1927—would prove a transitional one for the Englands.

Once more Harve took stock. He couldn't be a deputy forever. Though healthy, he wasn't getting any younger. He still had to make a living to support Hattie, Ruth, Rachel, and himself. Even with his deputy's pay, it was tight. If farming was to pay off, he needed more land. But, once more he would have to come up with the money to pay for it. Maybe it was just the time of year—dreary, gray, and cold. Shortly, warmer March weather and the clattering of geese overhead would herald spring and maybe a better mood.

Between checking seed catalogs, tending his egg layers, and performing his duties as deputy, Harve issued a call for hunters to rid the area of the wolves preying on farm animals near Burlington Junction. On the appointed Sunday, Harve carefully explained to the teams of hunters how and where the hunt was to be conducted. Unfortunately, it was not as successful as he had hoped. There was even a difference of opinion about whether a pack of three animals was coyotes, as he claimed, or wolves. A second Sunday hunt was planned, this time using only hound dogs, which proved no more successful in terms of capturing the wily animals.

Then there was a blur of events.

First, it was Sam's Savannah "Savages," which lost 13–8 to Maryville on February 10, but got revenge in a 21–19 squeaker a month later in the Northwest Missouri High School Basketball Tournament. However, they lost in the tournament finals, which Sam's parents faithfully attended.

Two weeks later, the courthouse clock—by which most Maryvillians kept time—stopped. That is, it stopped for eight minutes, and then the old mechanism went on a spree, gaining minutes. At 6:15 a.m. on March 23, it stopped again. Its one-ton, five-hundred-pound weights were given their weekly winding by janitor John H. Thorp, though the clock was then three hours behind Central Standard Time. Thorp said it was now up to clock repairman Paul Kuchs, who alone seemed to possess the mys-

tic powers to provide the correct setting. Once a cog was fixed,
Thorp reset the valued timepiece.

Daughter Ruth, despite working her way through school
like her brothers, was outdoing both of them. Before graduat-
ing, she would earn the letter "M" (smaller and less prestigious
than the men's) in varsity girls' soccer, volleyball, and basketball.
She also worked on the *Northwest Missourian* (the campus paper),
served as student council vice president, and was admitted to one
of the campus honor societies.

In mid-May, in common with millions, Hattie and Harve ea-
gerly followed reports of the solitary flight of the "Lone Eagle,"
Charles Lindbergh, across the ocean. His parting words rang in
their ears during those thirty-three and a half perilous hours:
"When I get into the cockpit, it's like getting a death sentence.
And if I get to Paris, it will be like a pardon from the governor."
He made it and was honored in the French and U.S. capitals.

On Monday, August 1, Howell and Sam returned flush
from National Guard summer camp at Fort Riley, Kansas, and
per agreement, eloped that same day. Howell took as his bride
pretty, black-haired Mildred ("Millie") Cooper, whom he had
met through a dorm friend of hers. (Revealing of Millie's re-
lationship with her in-laws, Harve was always and forever "Mr.
England," while her mother-in-law was "Hattie.") Sam married
Vera Clark, a vivacious redhead he had met at the college. The
brothers reasoned that they could not ask their parents to help
pay for a wedding. Predictably, Hattie was disappointed in the
absence of church weddings, but she took both daughters-in-law
to her bosom.

Unlike Harve, who seemed to have no interest, Hattie followed the infamous trial of shoemaker Nicola Sacco and fish
peddler, Bartolomeo Vanzetti. Accused of robbing and killing
a paymaster and guard at South Braintree, Massachusetts, the
immigrants had been convicted six years earlier. Protests of
their treatment had, like Lindbergh's flight, stretched across the
ocean. Nevertheless, shortly after midnight on August 27, they
were executed.

Harve was much more interested in the contest for the
home run title in the American League and the hot pennant

race his Cardinals were in again. The first race involved Babe Ruth, the Yankee slugger, and his teammate Lou Gehrig, who were neck and neck until early September. Then, in a tremendous burst, Ruth connected for four homers in four days, pushing his output to forty-eight, and finished the season with an unbelievable sixty. Like most, Harve was convinced no one would ever threaten Ruth's record.

Some afternoons, Harve stopped at Holt's to learn the fate of his Cardinals. Unfortunately, too often it seemed that the clerk spent most of his time twisting the radio dials trying to rid the static that drowned out the announcer. It seemed to be especially bad in the middle of September, when the Cards were in a crucial doubleheader with the Giants. As it turned out, Harve obtained some revenge when the eventual National League champions, the Pittsburgh Pirates, were shut out in the World Series by the Yankees in four games.

Sam's football team came to Maryville again in early November that year. Once more, Harve and Hattie tried to follow the action. Despite the efforts of Sam's husky captain and fullback, Victor Mahood, who scored a touchdown and passed to a teammate for the extra point, Sam's team managed only a tie. After the game, Sam dropped his glower long enough to greet his waiting parents.

The elder Englands were also there when Sam brought his cagers to the Maryville High School gym six weeks later. Sam's post-game mood was no better than it was the past November. His team had suffered a 17–16 loss to his alma mater. He wanted fiercely to do well in his hometown, knowing that the *Democrat-Forum* would report the results with his name prominent in the article.

Despite the fact that he didn't drive, the 1927 Ford caught Harve's attention. Introduced in August and claiming to attain a maximum speed of sixty-five miles per hour, it was a wonder. Called the Model A, it not only replaced the familiar "T," but was markedly different. A mere photograph of the inside, showing the steering wheel, dashboard and instruments, was enough to excite the car enthusiast. Its controls offered just about anything the driver could want. However, older drivers were in shock;—it had a hand gearshift. That would be too much to master. Uncharacteristically, Harve began talking about buying a two-seater! Hattie couldn't believe it.

Still, one of those fancy cars might be helpful. A lot of Harve's time and energy was devoted to chasing after moonshiners, who were getting cleverer, or more desperate, all the time. One night the sheriff was tipped off that a still was being operated outside Pickering, north of Maryville. After driving nearly eleven miles and searching fruitlessly for over an hour, Harve, Sheriff Campbell, Prosecuting Attorney Wright, and Deputy John Rasco discovered a half-barrel of sour mash behind a locked door and covered by several boxes and sugar stacks. Hidden even better was a still. A ten-gallon jar of clean corn mash had been secreted in a cave outside the house. Yet, the operator was nowhere in sight.

Harve tired of those nighttime forays and—though abstemious—hoped that the "Wets" might win the legislative battles and put an end to this whole business. He even began to think of resigning.

An excuse to do so arose in late July. R.F. Wallace offered for sale a five-acre tract in South Park, just across the road from Harve's and Hattie's house. Wallace wanted a staggering $2,500 (over $30,000 in 2015) for the land, but Harve decided to take the gamble. This would give him twenty-eight lots, or close to seven acres, which he could put into strawberries, raspberries, blackberries, and grapes. So, he struck the deal with Wallace. Apprized, but not really consulted, Hattie was pleased. Harve might now focus on farming, leaving it to others to administer the law. His resignation as deputy seemed to confirm her hope.

Two weeks later, the *Democrat-Forum* reported that Harve had decided to revive the Izaak Walton League, an environmental organization formed in 1922 that had been dormant for two years. Harve was a deputy game warden and national field representative for the League, and within only a few days of canvassing, produced twenty-five signatures, including Mayor Garrett's. By the third week in August, temporary chapter president Harve England announced twenty-five more members and the arrival of the charter from the national headquarters. The next steps were to obtain a game preserve and elect a permanent chapter president. Harve refused the nomination, stating, "A younger man is needed to energize the chapter, and I'll support him."

However, that was not the extent of his involvement. He captained one of the teams for the League rabbit hunt on December 20. The winning team was decided by a point system: fifteen points were awarded for each new member brought in to the chapter, seven points were awarded for a crow, owl, or hawk, and five points were awarded for a rabbit. The losers were obligated to treat the winners to a dinner the night after the hunt. Unfortunately, Harve's skills could not make up for his teammates' deficiencies, so he helped treat his good friend Walter Smith's winning team on the 21st.

Hattie's clock ticked out the old year and chimed in the new, and she admitted to herself that, except for the scorching heat that set records from July through October, it had been a good year. Her sons had married fine girls and were successful in their teaching careers. Ruth and Rach were home often enough to keep things lively, and Harve's purchase of the five acres and his resignation as deputy seemed to foretell a life more to her taste. Hattie prophesied that 1928 would be a good year.

Was she in for a surprise.

Chapter Six

Harve Drops a Bombshell

The year began uneventfully, though January was unusually mild, with the temperature hitting fifty-four degrees on the 9th. True to form, on February 2, the groundhog saw its shadow, portending another six weeks of winter.

Except for gasoline and eggs, prices were higher. Because of the mid-July hail and record heat, the previous fall's corn crop was only 59 percent of normal, and wheat only 63 percent. Combined with the high retail prices, it was a real concern. At 5¢ a pound, the price of butter was up 10 percent over the previous year and coffee was up 7¢ a pound, an almost 60 percent hike.

By contrast, the nation's bankers were optimistic, despite almost two million unemployed persons. Before the year was out, stocks would set a record of four million shares sold in one hour, with RCA the biggest seller, and General Electric hitting 144 7/8, a new high. By October, when General Motors climbed to $187 1/2 a share, the booming market was all the talk around town.

The "Wets" continued to press for repeal of Prohibition, countered by the nation's churches and the GOP generally.

Amelia Earhart, "Lady Lindy," became America's darling when she successfully piloted her plane to England. Her photograph graced the papers regularly, and Hattie enjoyed seeing a woman get her due.

Those who had radios were temporarily distressed when the Radio Commission reallocated broadcast wavelengths. What used to be WDAF in Kansas City at 370.2 became WEBH, and WHB at 336.9 was now WJAX. Similar changes occurred across the wavelengths from Boston to San Antonio. It seemed to Midwesterners that only Chicago's familiar WMAQ and WLS remained at their respective wavelengths.

March temperatures, like those in January, were unusually warm, reaching eighty-five degrees on the 21st and 22nd and causing Harve's fruit trees to bud too early. He dared not plant anything so soon. A sharp temperature drop could ruin them. But, to Hattie, nothing could be as ruinous as Harve's announcement.

In late February, Harve had dropped a bombshell—he intended to run for sheriff again. While Hattie was usually ahead of him, she wasn't this time. He had only seemed unusually restless.

Harve reasoned that even with the additional five acres he had bought last summer, it would be tough going. The economy and weather were so unpredictable. He had ricked and sold all the firewood he could, and his eggs wouldn't bring anywhere near the revenue he needed. Corn would cost an arm and a leg, and butchering the hogs brought to him and rendering the lard depended on the whims of customers.

By law Sheriff Campbell could not succeed himself, and having come in second last time around, Harve thought he had a good chance of getting elected.

While not happy about his decision to run, Hattie didn't challenge him. She was relatively content in the little house they had owned since coming to Maryville. Howell and Millie often visited on weekends. Sam was just down the road in Savannah, but before the year was out, he would be teaching physical education and coaching football in Jackson, diagonally across the state. Even then, he and Vera generally made it home for holidays in their new Whippet auto. Ruth and Rachie were still home, though Ruth would graduate this May and seek her fortune.

Hattie had another nagging concern. No, it was a full-blown irritation, which could adversely affect Harve if elected sheriff. A major highway now ran through town. Begun in 1924, boosters called the new two-thousand-mile paved road, "The

Broadway of America," or the "Saints' Trail," as originally it was to link St. Louis, Missouri, and St. Paul, Minnesota. Hattie saw nothing saintly about it. Nonetheless, it now threaded its way through town, marking a new era, a bigger Maryville—one with more cars and more strangers.

Promoters had proclaimed the benefits Maryville would reap from the greater trade fostered by a new highway. Other smaller towns were drying up, and their stores boarding up. Enthusiasm for the new highway had rivaled the excitement generated for the normal school, until then Maryville's proudest achievement.

The energized townsfolk had sprung into action, and formed numerous committees. The courthouse clock dials were washed, tin cans were picked up, unsightly lots cleared, speeches delivered, church suppers and fairs held to raise money—all in the hopes of convincing the commissioners of Maryville's fitness. Representatives from Maryville and rival towns had journeyed to St. Louis to make their cases.

U.S. Highway 71 was now a reality. While it did not live up to its promise to connect Maryville to either of the Saints, it offered a direct route between Kansas City to the south and Omaha to the north. However, Maryville was a mess for too long as men and equipment replaced the narrow road with the two-lane concrete strip. To make it worse, the road was less than three hundred yards east of Hattie's and Harve's property.

The Englands' lives would never be the same again. Trucks rumbled through town, carrying hogs down Highway 71 to the St. Joseph stockyards. Additionally, an auction barn, where livestock changed hands each Tuesday, had been built across the road from the Englands' house. The Poland China Association, which operated in three states, established their headquarters in Maryville and promoted the sale of their pedigreed hogs.

Although Hattie never expressed her feelings in so many words, she harbored doubts about what her husband would face as sheriff. Maybe Harve did as well, though he was just as characteristically unexpressive. Hattie wondered if Harve would be up to the new demands being laid on the town—and him—by the changes.

Hattie feared that more crime had come with the new highway. In fact, the past year had seen 202 arrests, an increase over the previous two years, in part due to greater traffic and strangers to the area. Up until now, most of the crimes were committed by locals, the vast majority by whites, and few of them involved violence. Nor were crimes committed by African Americans any more serious. The bulk of the 338 crimes committed by African Americans between 1919 and 1929 were bootlegging and gambling.

However, the only doubt Harve outwardly expressed about running for sheriff was whether he would have to put away his fishing poles and waders. That would be a real sacrifice.

On March 5, Harve walked uptown to County Clerk Fred Wright's office and plunked down the $5.00 filing fee. John Surplus, a Democrat from Ravenwood who too had been one of Campbell's deputies, filed soon after Harve and mistakenly claimed to be the first candidate. The *Democrat-Forum* clarified the issue and reminded readers that Harve had also been first to file four years ago. The paper then recalled that he had been "an officer of the law for many years": as a deputy under the two previous sheriffs, as Maryville's chief of police, and "at present as a special officer of the city."

Though he wasn't really a Democrat, Harve ran on the Democratic ticket both times. Truth is he wasn't really into politics in the usual sense. However, for the last half-century—since the Depression of 1873—generally only Democrats won county offices. Paradoxically, the GOP dominated in the presidential elections of the 1920s.

In short order, six others filed their candidacies, three challenging Harve on the Democratic ticket and three for the GOP nomination. Harve lost no time having $10.25 worth of campaign cards and stationery printed and allocating $5.00 for advertising. Stamps ran him another $2.00, and he bought five nickel cigars to pass out. It would cost him another $5.00 to hire a car to drive to the various campaign rallies around the county; volunteer drivers, including his sons, came free. However uncomfortable, he appeared with other candidates at picnics throughout the county. He was disappointed at the turnout in Clearmont, where he and seven other Democratic candidates worked the crowd, but he enjoyed watching Clearmont's baseball team play against Hopkins's town team after the speeches. He returned the next day, Democratic Day, to a larger crowd and a satisfying Maryville win over the home team. Unfortunately, Barnard's Democratic Day picnic four days later was marred by heavy rain and mud, which cut attendance.

The family pitched in to help Harve campaign, though it was pretty low keyed. Underage Ruth and Rachie delivered posters in town and at the college, Howell and Sam talked up the candidacy with their Battery C friends, and Harve made the usual rounds.

On March 20, in the midst of the campaign excitement, Hattie was felled by an unexplainable illness. No one could remember her being bedridden, even after delivering her four children. Harve and the girls were both upset and baffled. Dr. Ryan, who visited Hattie regularly and administered a variety of medicines without any noticeable results, was equally baffled. Hattie would get up and try to work, but she was back in bed the next day. Her sister Dora came down from Council Bluffs to help. Six weeks later, Dora was still there and filled in ("officiated" she called it) for Hattie at Rachie's high school graduation.

Painfully slowly, fifty-eight-year-old Hattie recovered, and by mid-summer she was largely back to normal. Dr. Ryan remained mystified over the cause. His medical knowledge (and that of the colleagues he consulted) was apparently too limited. He certainly claimed no credit for her recovery, however frequently he had looked in on her. Hattie's daughters would secretly attribute the mysterious illness to their father's candidacy.

On primary day, August 7, 1928, the Englands were understandably tense. Harve was clearly one of the favorites, but unofficial reports predicted some upsets. By 2:30 p.m., 962 voters from Polk Township (Maryville) had voted, of which close to a third came from Polk B, Harve's third ward. The Lanning Tire Shop, in the Martin building on South Main Street in the third ward, was a busy polling place. The turnout in Quitman, where Harve's sister Rachie and brother-in-law Bob still lived, was reported to be large also.

The Englands' worries proved groundless. Perhaps because his was the "closest contest," the *Democrat-Forum* headlined Harve's win, claiming that he "showed surprising strength." His 856 votes, though only a 94 plurality, represented the highest total of the eight candidates, Democratic and Republican. This assured him of the support of the county Democratic Party in his campaign against S.R. Dobbins, the Republican candidate from Barnard.

Harve also enjoyed some nice publicity from the *Democrat-Forum* when he was profiled by a reporter who regarded him as "quite a fellow." The reporter noted that in addition to his being a former police chief, a deputy sheriff, and member of the National Guard's Battery C, Harve had "developed a truck gardening business on his little place south of Maryville, which is one of the most unique one-man propositions in this part of the country." The reporter, who visited the farm, was amazed at all the candidate got out of just eight city lots. At the time four were in watermelons, three were in strawberries, muskmelons, and cantaloupes, and the remaining one was in pasture. Harve would also grow potatoes, beans, grapes, tomatoes, onions, beets, peas, turnips, and cucumbers on his small acreage. He even squeezed twenty-five cherry trees into one corner of his property. At other times he would have pears, peaches, raspberries, blackberries, and mulberries underway. Harve also prided himself on his hulless Japanese popcorn, according to the obviously sympathetic reporter. This was the kind of undertaking expected of a much younger man, not a sixty-year-old, however trim and healthy looking.

However, Harve didn't get off scot-free. He still had to shell out $132.50 for the general election. One hundred dollars went to the party. Advertising and business cards set him back $24.50, while cigars cost him $3.00 and "car hire" ran him $5.00.

Harve counted on voters to agree that he was, as the paper had put it, "quite a fellow," and translate this opinion into votes. For now, he and Hattie awaited the results, which were solemnly announced at the *Democrat-Forum* office after the polls closed on November 6.

Elsewhere, former Secretary of Commerce and presidential candidate, Herbert Hoover, closely watched election returns. The contest was billed as a test of the "Coolidge Prosperity." Indeed, Hoover prophesied, "We in America today are nearer to the final triumph over poverty than ever before in the history of the land." Voters were convinced. Though Al Smith picked up nearly twice the number of votes as the Democratic candidate in 1924, Hoover clobbered Smith in the electoral vote, grabbing almost 60 percent of the popular vote. In fact, Smith did not even take his own state. Even the normally Democratic Nodaway County went Republican.

On the other hand, Harve narrowly defeated GOP candidate S.R. Dobbins, 6,395 to 6,077. Equally narrowly, Paul "Pete" Jones, a NWMSTC and Missouri Law School graduate running on the GOP ticket, won the race for prosecuting attorney. Harve had followed this race almost as avidly as his own, for he would have to work closely with the prosecutor.

The newly-elected sheriff promptly secured the $15,000 bond from the American Security Company of New York, which was duly approved by circuit court judge, John Dawson. For all intents and purposes, he was ready for his new challenge. Maybe he would be able to play more Cribbage games.

The past decade in Maryville had been an exciting time for the Englands. Harve had found his niche. The England children had succeeded, as well. Sons Howell and Sam had ably navigated their way through the Maryville schools and college. Like their father, Howell's and Sam's achievements were duly reported in the *Democrat-Forum*. On December 19, Sam's entire letter to his parents was printed in the paper. Sam enthusiastically extolled the merits of the new gym at Jackson, near Cape Girardeau, and his basketball team, which had won its first game 45–4, despite practicing for only a week.

The *Democrat-Forum* editor also reported Ruth's accomplishments. This academic year she had been easily elected vice president of the student association at the college, served on the "secret" committee to plan the annual "walk out," and helped plan the party honoring the mothers of coeds at the college. Mrs. Harve had put on her finest to make her daughter proud at that

December 6 tea. Not to be outdone, Rachie had succeeded at the high school, winning some academic awards.

The two months after the election were busy ones for the Englands, as they organized for their move uptown to the jail and sold their little house. It would not be easy to leave their home. While tiny, it somehow managed to accommodate the whole family—Harve and Hattie, Howell and Millie, Sam and Vera, Ruth and Rachel—that Christmas. As always, Hattie was up to the occasion, her mysterious illness a thing of the past.

Memories of their move to Maryville came back with a rush. Now, Harve and Hattie, "Sheriff and Mrs. England," were entering a new phase of their lives, one that would be public—all too public—in the upcoming years. Hattie's clock, forever known as the "jail clock," would mark memorable events over the next four life-altering years.

Chapter Seven

The Englands Settle In

Having served as deputy for four years, Harve knew his way around the jail when he began his term January 1, 1929. He and Hattie would have to get used to living there, however. They would live in the front part of the first floor, which held a big dining room, a sizeable kitchen, and a comfortable living room. Male prisoners were held in the basement in a revolving cage (the outer bars holding the prisoners revolved, not the floor). Female prisoners, less frequent guests, were housed on the second floor.

Nodaway County Jail, ca. 1930

Throughout the four years, Hattie always seemed to have other boarders. Often they were family, like crippled cousin Doris Mitchell and addle-brained "Aunt" Mayme. But she also housed male college students, often athletes (including daughter Rachie's future husband), who earned their room and board. Along with prisoners charged with lesser crimes, they helped her clean the jail, cook, wash clothes, and mow the lawn—whatever needed to be done. The work was endless. One night Hattie made supper for eighteen, including six prisoners, after which she labored for two hours washing dishes.

In time Hattie became known as the "Great Protector" because of her thoughtfulness toward the less fortunate. However, her managerial skills were the real wonder. They were severely tested when she became, in daughter Rachie's words, "Innkeeper" at the jail.

Given the number of official and unofficial boarders for whom she cared, it is a wonder that she was able to stretch the jail budget as far as she did. Sewing a young prisoner's coat before he was released from the jail was typical of her thoughtfulness. Another time, a woman whose husband was in jail was herself arrested and jailed for stealing a coat from one of the clothing stores. Hattie helped her care for her baby and later, upon the woman's release, presented her with a new coat.

According to Rachie, Hattie's "best help" came from prisoners charged with what Hattie felt were minor offenses. With only 75¢ a day per prisoner, she had to be resourceful. She simply made more than a few prisoners "trustys," or, as daughter Ruth recalled, "spoiled them." Hattie had definite ideas about which prisoners would make good trustys, Rachie remembered, and at times those ideas clashed with "higher authorities." "Virg" was her favorite trusty. A relatively frequent cage occupant, he helped fix meals, spade the garden, and chop wood. He also was known to take advantage of her good nature, including one time when, in Hattie's own words, "he stole one on Mrs. Sheriff and slept upstairs" where family and boarders stayed. Another time he came back from a trip uptown on an errand for Hattie with some liquor for another prisoner. When Harve returned from a trip he had a few words with Hattie about that incident. She and Harve even allowed Virg's wife some marital privileges one time. And then there was the time that she and Harve took Virg to the movies with them.

Her daughters long remembered when Hattie first met Virg, a rural mail carrier. According to them, she asked the deputy who locked up Virg what he was in for. The deputy told her a year for drunken driving. "A year!" Hattie harrumphed. Sententiously, the deputy—whom she didn't care for—responded, "He'll have to be treated pretty rough. In for a year, you know, he'd run off in a minute if he had a chance." Apparently Hattie fumed, "I wonder whose fault it is was that a young man [with a young wife and daughter] like him learned to like liquor in the first place?"

But Hattie was far less charitable toward the deputy who had brought Virg in. She felt he was too self-important. She thoroughly enjoyed the time the deputy handcuffed himself to a prisoner, but couldn't open the cuffs when he returned to the jail. Tersely she wrote, "Ha Ha."

While Harve might disapprove of some of Hattie's management, he had to admit he needed her and her skills.

The year 1929 started calmly enough. In his inaugural address that March, President Hoover assured the nation that the future "is bright with hope." While there had been some signs that the bull market might not be sustainable, the markets still climbed. Hoover's reassurances seemed to buoy the spirits of investors. General Motors hit 150, followed the next day by Radio Corporation of America's 12 ¾ jump to 120 ½. Even careful Harve got caught up in the excitement and dipped a toe into the investment stream. On July 1, he purchased one share of preferred and four shares of Nodaway Milk Products Company common stock.

However, news from across the Atlantic was disturbing. Reports of riots in Berlin and the rising strength of the fascists were reminders of a war that had destroyed so many lives and futures. War hero Von Hindenburg, the German president, seemed helpless to resist domination by the fascists. Mahatma Gandhi's example of passive resistance to British rule was virtually ignored.

Nonetheless, efforts to assure a peaceful world had resulted in the ratification of the Kellogg-Briand Treaty in 1927, which outlawed war and was named for the French foreign minister and U.S. secretary of state. Though it would prove futile, the effort was reinforced by Erich Maria Remarque's 1928 book, *All Quiet on the Western Front,* which would be translated into English in 1929, and made into a popular movie. War's cruelty rather than heroism was forcefully demonstrated by the German soldiers. Buster Keaton's *Doughboys* took a different tack.

Yet, preparedness remained a concern. During the summers, Battery C of Maryville's National Guard trained at Fort Riley, Kansas, typically receiving "very satisfactory" ratings from the federal inspector and winning a number of prizes. For example, in 1930 the three-man machine gun squad would take second place with fifty-six points out of one hundred. (One has to wonder how successful the first place squad was!) The eight-man French .75 gun squad was almost as proficient, if that is the correct word. The battery commander, Captain Edward Condon, was proud of his "boys," a collection of locals, college students, and alumni.

Mainly the new sheriff focused on the job at hand. He readily acclimated to the job, for which he had unknowingly been preparing the past half dozen years or so. Initially he appointed two deputies: C.G. (Grant) McMillen, former Pickering postmaster, and George Rimel, who like Harve, had presided over the Northwest Missouri Poultry Association. He would later appoint Robert Jones, who ran a sand and gravel business in Maryville, and Johnny Behm, who did much of the driving for Harve. Curiously, their seeming lack of law enforcement experience was not an issue.

Harve seemed to be out more at night. Car wrecks, stills, and petty thefts occupied a lot of time—always at the wrong time of day, it seemed. Hattie marked time with her Sessions mantel clock. It could be lonely in that big, cold jail. While her husband was out, Hattie would hear the clock strike the hour or half hour. Sometimes, however, it seemed the hands stood still. She would anxiously listen for his car to drive up or the jail door to open, indicating his safe arrival. If she had her way, the deputies would do more of the night work. Meanwhile her clock ticked away.

Like the county itself, Maryville was growing. Nearly a fifth of the county, 5,217 people, called Maryville home. The population reflected the demography of the county, with an almost equal number of males and females, a small number of foreign born, and a much smaller number of African Americans. The latter represented only a fraction of the population, only ninety-five in the whole county. Politically, the county was strongly Democratic, though it would elect two Republicans to county office later in the year. Schizophrenically, the county tended to vote Republican for national offices.

The *New York Sun* later would proclaim what county residents already touted: "Agriculturally, Nodaway County is one of the richest in Missouri." Dotted with thriving villages, it boasted of good school facilities, including a college in Maryville, and an adult population that was "100 per cent. English reading."

However, the local paper was less optimistic. It reported that residents were concerned about whether to spend more than $300,000 on county roads during these perilous times. After over-expanding to meet WWI demand for more food, farm prices were now dropping, but mortgage payments were not. While building county roads would mean more jobs, some folks simply opposed spending public money on anything. They already feared bank failures, which might wipe out what small savings they had.

Then came what later would be called a "Perfect Storm." On October 24, U.S. Steel, which had sold at 205 ½, slid to 193 ½; General Electric, which had traded at 400 a few weeks earlier, dropped to 315. Still, few investors were ready for Tuesday, October 29, when the crash came. There was bedlam on the New York Stock Exchange as investors tried to sell their stocks before they dropped any farther. By the end of the month, twenty-five billion had been lost. Warning signs had been there—overproduction of capital and goods, excessive expansion, installment buying, and depressed European trade—but they had mostly been ignored.

Banks failed, brokerages folded, and unemployment visited too many homes. Three of Nodaway County's major banks closed. Additionally, grasshoppers would destroy fields of grain in Iowa, Minnesota, Nebraska, and the Dakotas. Wheat prices would drop to historic lows. Especially troubling was the general air of uncertainty.

Even so, as 1930 dawned, there was little to mark the beginning of Sheriff England's second year in office. Arrests in 1929 were down to 62 from 154 in 1927 and 131 in 1928. Fourteen arrests were for liquor violations and ten arrests were for forgery and larceny, signs of the times. Before the year was out, Harve and his deputies would make another thirteen arrests, ranging from murder and first-degree manslaughter to larceny. There was even an escape when a deputy's attention was diverted. The prisoner, arrested for murder, took off. Harve promptly called the Buchanan County sheriff in St. Joe to alert him to look for the escapee. Shortly, there was a call that the prisoner had been brought in; Harve could pick him up any time. There was no urgency, however, because—strangely—the prisoner was not considered all that dangerous. Nor was he likely to go any place soon.

Harve and deputies, l to r: John Behm, Robert E. Jones, Sheriff England,
Cash Whitman, C. G. (Grant) McMillen

Minor excitement was generated by the arrival of the new deputy county clerk, forty-year-old Clyde Perkins. As long as anyone could recall, the 570-pound Perkins had been called "Fatty." He had learned to accept it good-naturedly, and was the first to laugh when his weight caused a barber chair to collapse. The county bought a special chair to accommodate him. Despite his bulk, his chest measuring 59½ inches and his waist, 68½ inches, Perkins did his job well. In fact, he was considered an expert accountant, which would lead to his being elected county treasurer. Hattie enjoyed his laughter, which seemed to bubble up from deep in his stomach and explode at something funny.

She derived much greater satisfaction from the births of two "babes," the first England grandchildren. Howell's and Millie's son, John Harvey England, came into the world in mid-July that year. Sam's and Vera's daughter, Elaine, arrived four months later. Hattie, who had waited a long time for grandchildren, was joyous. Each visit of the grandchildren was an event.

When time hung heavy, Harve would walk over to Warren Jones's drugstore on the north side of the square. An old friend from their Quitman days, Warren not only dispensed prescriptions, but bits of wisdom and humor. Harve could relax with Warren. He was no longer Sheriff England; rather, he was just Harvey.

Warmer weather meant baseball. Whenever he had the time, Harve would tune in his big Crosley radio to listen to his St. Louis Cardinals. (He had given in and bought the radio, which in time became a comfort to him and Hattie.) Under the new manager, Gabby Street, the team started where it left off the previous year—losing. Unhappy with manager Bill McKechnie, general manager Branch Rickey had dumped him halfway through the 1929 season. McKechnie's replacement, Billy Southworth, once a favorite, was no more successful. But, even with the change of managers, it looked just as bad for the Cards' fans.

By mid-August, Harve's Cardinals were ten games behind the Chicago Cubs. Manager Street didn't seem any better than McKechnie or Southworth. Then, miraculously, the Cards came alive. Spitballer Burleigh Grimes, who was obtained from Boston in June (and who would win thirteen games), was turning things around. Left fielder Chick Hafey was hitting around .336. Before the season was over, sparkplug Frankie Frisch would surpass him in average and runs batted in. The redbirds won thirty-eight of the next forty-eight games. On the last day of the season, with the Cards one game ahead of the Cubs, rookie pitcher Jerome Dean debuted with a 3–1 win. (The "Dizzy" one would go on to a highly successful baseball career before entertaining fans and driving English teachers crazy with his convoluted syntax, e.g. "the runner slud into third base.")

Though the Cards would lose the World Series 4 games to 2 to Connie Mack's Philadelphia Athletics, which batted a lowly .197, Harve and other Cardinal fans were pleased. The Cardinals were back, and rumors were that they would be better next year.

The Englands also followed the college football team, the Bearcats, though they still didn't understand the game. They were there to see a rising star, Victor Mahood—a swarthy, black-haired sophomore from Savannah, who had taken an interest in daughter Ruth. He had worked on farms growing up, and after briefly dropping out of high school, labored in the construction of Highway 71. His high school coach, Sam England, had encouraged him to enroll at Sam's alma mater. There, the young man's football prowess could be put to good use. At 185 muscular pounds, Mahood was a rugged tackle on defense and a speedy fullback on offense.

However, the Bearcats gained more attention from their off-the-field activities, which led to their being called "Lefty Davis and the 40 Thieves," borrowing from the folk tale "Ali Baba and the 40 Thieves." It seems that on away trips to football games Coach Davis's team had sticky fingers.

Hattie continued to maintain order in the jail. She boarded the inmates, worked her "trustys" and college students—including Rachie, when she could pin her down—and entertained relatives. Of course, nothing compared to visits from daughter Ruth, who was teaching in St. Joseph, and her sons, daughters-in-law, and their "babes."

Maryville, like the rest of the nation, began feeling the effects of what was being called a depression, in time the Great Depression. Bank failures were troubling, but nothing was as devastating as losing one's job or house to foreclosure. By the end of 1931, there were foreclosures on thirty-five farms near Maryville, the most in memory. Rents on property in and around Maryville were in arrears up to three years. Nationally, unemployment would soon surpass two million, and eventually reach 25 percent. Farm prices fell. Some dairy farmers dumped their milk rather than sell at such diminished prices. A Kansas farmer dumped a truck filled with wheat onto a street rather than sell his crop for 27¢ a bushel. While Maryville didn't suffer to the extent of other parts of the country, there was nothing they could do when the banks closed their doors and wiped out their savings. Ten banks in the county would close between 1928 and 1931. The *Democrat-Forum* editor, recognizing the anxiety many felt, called for "cooler heads" to have more confidence in the banks and the economy generally.

Despite the financial woes that affected so many, 1930 began innocently enough for Harve. There was a bit of a scare in mid-October, in St. Genevieve over on the Mississippi River. Louis Ribeau, a black mail carrier, had been charged with armed robbery along with two other men. He had been seized by a mob, but escaped. Meanwhile nine members of the mob were arrested by the county sheriff and deputies. Three days later, on October 15, the governor called out the National Guard to prevent a mob from freeing the men accused of kidnapping Ribeau. However, after the kidnappers' five hundred dollar fines and sixty-day jail sentences were stayed, racial tension remained high. The Justice Department in Jefferson City opened an investigation for possible civil rights violations, the punishment for which was five thousand dollars, ten years in jail, or both.

Then there was seeming quiet; the Justice Department investigations came to naught. It was a reminder of Missouri's— the nation's—history of violence and ambivalence toward civil rights.

For the most part, Missouri had been spared the fate of its neighbor "Bloody Kansas," but it had known violence. Bordering Kansas, Missouri inevitably was drawn into the pitched battles and atrocities resulting from the Kansas-Nebraska Act of 1854, which permitted the admission of territories with or without slavery. Pro- and anti-slavery forces clashed. Bushwhacking, massacres, and raids on houses, farms, and businesses, were all too frequent. By June, open warfare had erupted. Even in 1862, after Union troops had chased the organized Confederates out, guerilla warfare continued. The most notorious guerillas were William Quantrill's raiders, whose targets were mostly pro-Union civilians. And for fifteen years, Jesse and brother Frank, former guerillas and sons of a minister and founder of William Jewel College, gained a reputation for their bank and train robberies.

More serious were the Bald Knobbers, who terrorized southwestern Missouri for almost a decade, beginning in 1883, and offered a model for vigilantes. Formed to combat lawlessness, this group eventually became as feared as those they were to combat. For example, shortly after forming, approximately one hundred Bald Knobbers broke into a jail, kidnapped brothers accused of wounding a shopkeeper, and hanged them. Other targets were "lowlifes" (drunks, gamblers, and "loose women"), wife beaters, and even the "ornery." Flogging, hanging, or beating became commonplace punishments. However, as violence escalated, anti-Bald Knocker groups formed. By 1889, after some bloody melees, the Bald Knockers slowly disappeared. But this was southwest, not northwest, Missouri.

Lynching, of which there was a small increase in 1930, had very different origins. Virginia's Colonel Charles Lynch is credited with the first "lynching." Initially, it took the form of local informal "courts," convened to deal with criminals and Tories on the frontier during the American Revolution. Punishments were usually fines and whippings. As it spread west, "lynch-law" (extra-legal judicial administration) was applied mostly to horse thieves and desperados.

During and after the Civil War, lynching took its more familiar form—killings by mobs. Initially, more whites than blacks were victims. For example, from 1882 to 1888 the ratio was 595 whites to 440 blacks. By 1892, the ratio was virtually even: 69 whites to 62 blacks. However, ten years later more than 100 blacks a year were lynched, and from 1906 to 1915, the ratio of blacks to whites was ten to one.

The usual rationale for lynching was to do "justice" to African Americans alleged to have raped white women. However, of a reported 3,811 lynchings between 1889 and 1941, less than 17 percent of the victims were even accused of rape. In fact, most lynchings were for quite minor "offenses," e.g., threatening to sue a white, attempting to register to vote, or "being disrespectful." A Georgia woman was hanged and burned for simply threatening to name the killer of her husband.

Hangings were the most common form of lynching, and they were often preceded by extreme brutality. In 1893, a hot poker was used to gouge out a black man's eye before he was burned. Thirty years later, a black man was chained to a log and barbequed. Castration before the hanging or burning was a favored punishment by some mobs. Afterwards, souvenir hunters would scramble for "prizes."

Some southern politicians seemed to pride themselves on their ability to incite lynchings. In 1914, South Carolina's Senator Benjamin ("Pitchfork Ben") Tillman declared he "would lead a mob to lynch any man...who ravaged a woman, black or white." Late nineteenth century Georgia Congressman and presidential candidate Tom Watson declared that lynchings and floggings were signs that justice prevailed.

As late as the 1920s, lynching remained a part—albeit a dark one—of American life. In March 1927, a mob bent on lynching three black men accused of assaulting two white girls was met by an equally angry section of the black community in Coffeyville, Kansas. The would-be lynchers tried to storm the "colored" section of the county jail but were met by stones and shotguns, causing a number of injuries. The rioting forced the local authorities to call in the National Guard, which finally imposed martial order using weapons and tear gas. Two months later, Southeast Missouri's Pemiscot County sheriff and his black prisoner were less fortunate. The jail was stormed, and the mob dragged the prisoner to another town where he was hanged. The sheriff escaped serious harm, but not every lawman was so lucky. A South Carolina sheriff was hospitalized a month earlier after being overpowered by a mob of two hundred, which took the black prisoner two miles out of town where he was found "riddled with bullets."

While lynchings were on the decline nationally, in 1930 there was a minor, but unexpected, rise. The Commission on Interracial Cooperation counted twenty-one lynchings, up from ten in 1929, eleven in 1928, and sixteen in 1927. No reason was given for the increase, though there was a feeling that the Depression was causing stress and leading to forms of "self-help" or emotional release. Twenty of those lynched were African Americans, sixteen of whom were taken from lawmen or killed within jails. But, if Sheriff England was aware of these statistics, he could have discounted them as a southern phenomenon. Six of the lynchings were in Georgia and four in Mississippi.

The past February, a black man from Ocilla, Georgia, charged with murder and rape never even made it to the jail after his capture. A mob met the sheriff outside of town and forced him to drive as told. When he attempted to drive off the highway, the mob fired a shot that hit the car's gas tank, windshield, and doors, forcing the sheriff to stop. The sheriff was then compelled to watch the hour and a half torture and eventual burning of the captive. Two other brutal lynchings occurred in Georgia, despite attempts by sheriffs to protect the prisoners.

In Sherman, Texas, a black man had been placed in a vault in the courthouse. A mob burned the courthouse, took the body from the vault, carried it into the "colored section" of town, and burned the body. A Chickasha, Oklahoma, black man was shot in his jail cell by a mob, taken to a hospital where he was refused treatment, returned to the jail, and stabbed to death there.

The latest lynchings were in Indiana, America's heartland. On August 7, 1930, three teenage boys were arrested for the murder of a man and the rape of his date. After intense questioning, the three confessed and were locked in the Grant County jail in Marion. That night, a crowd stormed the jail, shouted, "Get 'em. Kill the niggers," and battered the doors off the hinges. The sheriff unsuccessfully tried tear gas. Two were hanged after being brutally beaten, while the third was released after an alibi was introduced.

Most Maryville residents, including Sheriff England, couldn't imagine anything similar happening in their town. Yes, there were some malcontents in the area. In February 1922, the *Democrat-Forum* reported that some 1,300 persons attended the meeting in St. Joseph of Klan No. 1, Knights of the Ku Klux Klan. The organizer of the hour-long meeting talked about the organization's ideals, its chief principle of "white supremacy," and the need to preserve the purity of American womanhood. The next month, there was a brief report that an organizer had been to Maryville. (Organizers reportedly returned a year later at a meeting attended by an estimated 125 persons.) Then in May, another story had it that the Maryville KKK was responsible for a letter threatening the managers of a traveling show near St. Joseph. True or not, the Buchanan County (St. Joseph) sheriff took it seriously and began investigating. Shortly thereafter, the St. Joseph police reported KKK threats from Savannah, just to the north. The following year, KKK officials just south of Maryville threatened to take matters into their hands if an eighteen-year-old black man was not convicted of assaulting a white girl. Giving those in Maryville reason to be nervous, two Maryville men, signing letters with the letters "KKK," demanded money from local businessmen. Police Chief England's prompt arrests of the letter writers eased the tension. Whether the KKK ever gained a real toehold in Missouri, as it had in Indiana, is unclear.

Sheriff England and others in Maryville saw little reason to fear anything untoward. Maryville had experienced only two murders in the past fifty years. And just five years earlier, Raymond Gunn, from one of the oldest black families in Maryville, had been defended by L. Amasa Knox at the request of the local branch of the NAACP. Though no confession was extracted from Gunn, a female student at the Northwest Missouri State Teachers College identified him as the man who had threatened her. Gunn was convicted and given a four-year prison sentence beginning on November 8, 1925. After the trial, Knox was quoted as saying that the good citizens of Maryville had shown him and Gunn, every courtesy, despite sharp feelings on the case. He was even quoted as commenting about "the feelings between the races [in Maryville] being better than most cities in Missouri."

Chapter Eight

Velma Colter

Between 6:00 p.m. and 7:00 p.m. on Tuesday, December 16, 1930, the phone rang at the jail. Velma Colter, a young schoolteacher at the rural Garrett School, had been found dead. Paul Ward, the son-in-law of the family with whom the victim boarded, called reporting the murder to Sheriff England. He then elaborated for the sheriff's benefit. Ward's father-in-law, T.H. Thompson, became concerned when the young teacher had not returned from school at the usual time. He grabbed his lantern and, accompanied by his dog, walked about half a mile to the school. Opening the door, he saw Miss Colter's clothes on the floor. Once inside, he spotted the body and quickly left the building. On his way home, Thompson hailed Fred Schooler and two others to tell them "our school teacher has been murdered." Once home, he revealed the gruesome news to Ward, who then called England.

The sheriff notified his deputies and summoned Dr. Charles D. Humberd, the county coroner. He then climbed into his car and rode southwest of town to the one-room, white clapboard building, where, shortly before 7:00 p.m., he met Ward.

Word of the shocking and frightful incident had already spread, as individuals picking up the phone on party lines heard the news. Astonishingly, to reach the school, Sheriff England and his deputies had to wend their way through a parade of automobiles. Once there, England and the deputies struggled to hold back the growing crowd of curious onlookers. Only Coroner Humberd was allowed through and into the building.

At first glance, there was nothing unusual about the school. Located at the intersection of a crossroads, it bore the name of W.T. Garrett, a former mayor and the father of Maryville's current mayor. Inside, the configuration fit the rigidity of the prevailing pedagogy. The teacher's desk was in the back of the room, keeping watch over rows of compact desks bolted to the floor.

Spoiling reminders of the approaching holiday season—scattered decorations and "Merry Christmas" neatly printed in large letters inside a holly wreath on the blackboard—was the body of pretty, blond-haired, twenty-year-old Velma Fern Colter. She was lying in a pool of blood in front of the door, her face and body mutilated.

A graduate of Maryville High School's class of 1928 and classmate of Rachel England, Colter had taken thirty hours of coursework at the college to obtain her teaching certification and had been in her first year of teaching. The school, operated by the college, was considered a model rural school and had been featured in various educational publications.

Sheriff England immediately began searching for indicators of the assailant's identity. The principal clues were reports of a man "skulking" in the vicinity both that afternoon and the previous one. William New, who was out plowing a field around 3:45 p.m. on Monday afternoon, reported seeing a man standing approximately fifty yards from the school. The man had hung around for roughly an hour until Miss Colter started toward the Thompsons' house, a half mile south of the school. The man had continued down the same road behind the young teacher, who ran the rest of the way. New didn't know whether she ran from fright or cold.

One of the Garrett School pupils also had seen a man Monday afternoon—and frightened—had run home. After learning of Miss Colter's death, his parents called Prosecuting Attorney Paul R. ("Pete") Jones, a former college football coach and friend of the Englands. It is unclear what Jones learned from the boy, but another boy provided possibly useful details: the man he saw wore a duck coat and cap. Other reports were too vague to be of any help.

Fighting a crowd that reportedly grew to nearly five hundred, making evidence collection more difficult, Harve worked through the cold night. (The sensationalism of the papers makes this number and many other details about the case suspect.) Bloodhounds from Savannah were brought in around 9:00 p.m. They entered the school with Sheriff England, Prosecutor Jones, Prosecutor-elect Virgil Rathbun, and Coroner Humberd.

It was a madhouse around the school. The crowd's curiosity gave way to irritation as Sheriff England and the others methodically examined the schoolroom. Crowd mutterings became criticisms of the sheriff; criticisms became threats. The sheriff tried to calm the crowd by announcing that he was being as thorough as possible and would shortly put the bloodhounds on the scent. When the two dogs began tracking, the crowd quieted down. But the dogs, which fought their way through the milling throng, lost the scent around midnight.

Eleven members of the National Guard's Battery C, led by Lieutenant H.F. ("Shorty") Lawrence, volunteered to help the sheriff after learning about the crowd threatening the investigation. Sheriff England deputized them and placed them strategically.

Meanwhile, around 10:30 p.m., Coroner Humberd dutifully called on six individuals to function as the "coroner's jury" and observe the murder scene. Humberd led the six into the schoolroom to look at the nude body. It was a gruesome sight. Humberd explained that bruises on Miss Colter's hand indicated that she had resisted her assailant. Some desks, normally bolted to the floor, had been displaced. The young teacher's head appeared to have been struck five times. Her nose and cheekbone were broken. Gashes, apparently from a knife, scarred her face and neck. Humberd then adjourned the jury until December 19, when they would hear the evidence formally.

Though figuring the killer was still close by, Sheriff England called on authorities in other towns to look for suspects. Quickly, suspects were rounded up as far away as Sedalia, Missouri, over one hundred miles southeast, and Shenandoah, Iowa, fifty miles northwest. Before hopping into his car at 5:00 a.m. on Wednesday, December 17, the sheriff had called St. Joseph's Chief of Detectives, John T. Duncan, to request help. As a larger city, St. Joe had specially trained investigators. Duncan sent two detectives, Tom Burnett and John Reichen, and a special investigator, B.T. Andrews. Andrews arrived around 10:30 a.m.

Even earlier, shortly after daylight, H.G. Strumphfer and his son put their bloodhounds on the trail again. The hounds led them almost a half mile south of the school—through two gates, into a cornfield, and to the back door of a farmhouse, near where William New had seen the man. The Strumphfers pulled the dogs back and tried again. Once more the hounds led them to the farmhouse. After circling the house, the dogs went east again, but as they had earlier, lost the scent. Investigators assumed that the dogs had picked up the scent of the man New had seen Monday afternoon when plowing.

That morning, Special Investigator Andrews focused on the schoolhouse itself, looking for incriminating fingerprints. Fortuitously, one of the National Guardsmen found footprints. The trade name, "Double Wear," appeared faintly. With his handy pocketknife, England carefully lifted the footprints from the frozen mud and preserved them in ice later that night. That day, three boys also found some bloody underclothing behind a railroad fence near Conception, some eighteen miles east of Maryville. Deputy Gabe Purcell, to whom the boys gave it, turned it over to Prosecutor Jones. Snow that night threatened, but did not stop, the evidence gathering.

Still in search of suspects, England appealed to the hunters who had been near the school the afternoon of the murder to identify themselves and help solve the crime. Subscriptions were being taken to raise a five hundred dollar reward fund.

The sheriff and prosecutor carefully pieced together what they had: on Tuesday, December 16, Miss Colter had dismissed her pupils at about 3:45 p.m. and stayed a while longer to finish various jobs. Witnesses claimed seeing the schoolhouse door open, but differed as to the timing. As far as the investigators could tell, it appeared that the assailant had surprised Miss Colter, beaten and knifed her, and dragged her body toward the door.

The sheriff wondered whether the killer was still there when the witnesses saw the open door.

The murder of the shy, but popular, young woman seemed not only senseless, but unbelievable. The horror was accentuated by a photograph that soon appeared in the *Maryville Daily Forum*. Below the tightly-waved, sculptured, blond hair was a pleasant face with captivating eyes. A necklace and locket above her lace collar hinted that the photo was likely taken at the time of Miss Colter's high school graduation.

In that day's paper, the editor had wondered what kind of fiend ("moron" was one label) could have killed the diminutive teacher. Fear alternated with frustration among residents as they awaited an arrest. The *Daily Forum* reported that a "pall has spread over the county." Fearing for their lives, women now locked doors and left lights on at night. Rural teachers promptly left their schools when the pupils did, and one even informed her pupils not to expect her before they arrived at 8:30 a.m. Some persons, chafing at the slowness of the authorities to arrest the killer, openly expressed their dissatisfaction. This sense of unease led the *Daily Forum's* editor to caution readers not to "become excited and overanxious because an arrest is not made the first 24 hours."

Meanwhile, Coroner Humberd assembled his jury (Banner Brummett, L.C. Foreman, Ben Chandler, Raymond Groves, E.F. Nagee, and F.W. Salveson). Brummett, rather than the more aptly named Foreman, was selected as foreman. Coroner Humberd had them view the body again and presented what evidence he had. Wearily, Sheriff England and the others continued to study the scarce clues.

Thursday evening, December 18, Prosecutor Jones brought in for questioning two boys whose trap lines had been discovered near the schoolhouse. A trapper's knife would have been the perfect weapon for the cuts on Miss Colter's body. However, lacking anything to connect them with the murder, they were promptly released.

Meanwhile, Sheriff England had alerted local authorities, including the newly-appointed special city officer Leo Atherton. On December 19, Officer Atherton spotted Raymond Gunn, his brother Ted, and Paul "Shike" Smith hunting in a field northeast of Gunn's parents' home on East Fourth Street. The officer casually stopped to talk with the men, noting Gunn's bloodied duck coat. Gunn explained that the coat had been bloodied by the rabbits they had just shot. Recalling Gunn's reputation and his current charge of carrying a concealed weapon, Atherton calmly asked them to unload their guns and drove the compliant men to town for questioning.

At 12:30 p.m., the sheriff quietly escorted Gunn into Prosecutor Jones's counsel room in the courthouse. Characterized as tight-lipped and steeled by frequent run-ins with the law, Gunn was questioned for about two and a half hours. At 3:15 p.m., Jones called in a stenographer. Despite England's attempts to hide Gunn's identity, reporters were watching events closely and sensed an arrest was about to be made. Late editions of the local papers announcing developments in the case were being prepared.

Behind closed doors, the prosecutor, sheriff, and investigators from St. Joseph (O.H Reichen, T.V. Burnett, and B.T. Andrews) confronted Gunn with a plaster cast of the heel print that the sheriff had dug up and refrigerated. It matched the heavy overshoes found on the rear stoop of his parents' house. The label "Double Wear," stamped on the bottom of the shoe and the heel, beveled from long use, was clearly visible. Gunn held to his innocence. Yes, he had been near the school the previous night; he often was, hunting or checking his traps. And yes, he had been near the school the next afternoon, near the time of the killing. Prosecutor Jones and Sheriff England pressed him for more details. Largely, they were going on his stained reputation, rumors, and a report by a car driver that he had seen Gunn near the school on the night of the murder.

At about 7:30 p.m., Prosecutor Jones recalled the stenographer, who remained for about an hour. Reporters were getting anxious. Was or wasn't there a confession? Neither the sheriff nor the prosecutor gave them any satisfaction.

At about 9:45 p.m., the door opened and the persistent reporters from the *Maryville Daily Forum* and the *St. Joseph News-Press* spotted Investigator Andrews chained to Raymond Gunn.

This was the tip-off to the reporters, who concluded Gunn must have confessed—or at least an arrest had been made. Then, just as abruptly, Gunn was spirited away to St. Joseph for his protection. The reporters immediately pressed for details.

An investigator for the Southern Commission on the Study of Lynching remarked that Prosecutor Jones had learned a lesson from Gunn's previous arrest for rape. Then Gunn was "beaten up badly," but never confessed. This time they "tried religion on him."

Raymond Gunn, born January 11, 1904, was the oldest of Em and Mamie Gunn's eight children. Em was from one of the well-regarded pioneer black families in the county. After attending Douglass School through seventh grade, Raymond worked as a cook and "houseman" for Maryville families. Though a commission investigating the murder claimed that Gunn was "simply born 'with a bad streak,'" the few reports on him were generally positive. As the son of a Mason, he had attended at least some Masonic activities as "Master Raymond." The "first serious trouble," according to the investigator, was his imprisonment on an assault charge in 1925. He was released approximately twenty-one months early because of "merit time" and "jail time." A prison description that he was "considered a 'smart nigger'... quicker and brighter than most of the colored prisoners," did Gunn no favor.

On May 1, 1928, approximately four months after his release from prison, Gunn married Valdora (or Vandora) Kelley and moved to Omaha. A common rumor, according to the commission investigator, was that she died shortly thereafter due to Gunn beating her and kicking her in the chest, rather than pneumonia. Back in Maryville in 1930, Gunn obtained hunting and trapping licenses, a relatively common way members of the black community made money.

On December 19, witnesses T.H. Thompson, Coroner Humberd, and Detective Reichen testified at the coroner's inquest, held in the circuit court room. The papers summarized the jury's verdict and trumpeted their own verdict: twenty-six-year-old Raymond Gunn had killed Velma Colter.

Maryville Daily-Forum, *January 12, 1931*

Raymond Gunn

That same day, Velma Colter was buried. Maryville's First Methodist Episcopal Church was filled to capacity well before the 1:30 p.m. service. In fact, many had filed by the bier at 11:00 a.m. or 1:00 p.m. A mass of flowers adorned her white coffin. A barely opaque white cloth was stretched over the open casket to hide evidence of the young woman's wounds. Promptly at 1:30 p.m., a mixed quartet began the service with a rendition of "Beautiful Isle of Somewhere":

Somewhere the sun is shining
Somewhere the songbirds dwell
Hush, then my sad repining
God lives, and all is well.
Somewhere. Somewhere. Beautiful Isle of Somewhere.

The words of this old and familiar hymn, intended to offer the Colters solace, seemed appropriate on the sunny winter day. Reverend LaRue assured the Colters that their ill-starred daughter was now in God's hands, like their son who was killed in the Great War. The family had suffered enough, and they were unsettled, glum, and unforgiving.

At one point during the service, the mood changed. Rev. LaRue switched from extolling the "ambitious, pure, noble girl" to castigating the "licentious, impure and wicked person" who had caused her death.

Almost ghoulishly, the next day the *Daily Forum* reported, "Several Ask for Job as Teacher of Garrett School." One applicant was from Indiana and another from as far away as Bethany, West Virginia. The effects of the Depression clearly were being felt—a job was a job. However, given the circumstances and the fact that the school served only five pupils, authorities closed it.

With the prisoner safely locked away in the larger, more modern St. Joseph jail, Detective Reichen, the principal interrogator, painstakingly revealed the results of Gunn's questioning. Gunn had confessed, which the *Daily Forum* was quick to point out had been obtained without violence. The local newspapers sensationally reported the details of the confession. Gunn had been out near the school on Monday night, the night before the murder. He had hidden behind a cottonwood tree and watched the young teacher. The next evening, he had approached the building from the rear. Though he had picked up a three- to four-foot club, there had been no intent to kill.

Instead, he simply watched Miss Colter grade papers. When she finished, she carried a coal scuttle toward the door and opened it. She screamed at the sight of Gunn, who then grabbed her wrist and jerked her back into the room. She slipped away from him, thrust a broom at him, and attempted to retreat to the safety of her desk in the back of the room. The five-foot-seven, 142-pound Gunn grabbed her again. The young teacher bit his thumb and grabbed the coal scuttle to hit him, but Gunn struck her with the club. The young teacher fell against a desk before slumping on the floor. Gunn then dragged her body into the aisle between the desks.

Thinking Colter dead, Detective Reichen continued, Gunn was startled to hear her ask for a drink of water and say that her father would be looking for her. He then struck her with the club again, and appalled by what had happened, ran from the building.

But he soon returned and struck what may have been the fatal blow. The *Daily Forum* reported that Gunn then looked through the wire-grated windows for an opportunity to safely depart. When he spied a girl riding by on her horse, he ducked back from the window. Moments later, he fled toward town, retracing his steps and dropping the bloody club along the way.

A *St. Joe News-Press* editor, who at times accentuated the gorier details, wrote: "Not content with mere murder, the killer abused and mutilated the girl's body, stripping off most of her clothing." Then he had attempted to mop up the blood with the victim's coat, and failed to dispose of the body out of fear that someone would see him.

Detective Reichen said that Gunn stopped only once on his return trip—to break the ice in a small creek and ineffectively wash the blood from his glove. Then he went to his parents' Fourth Street home.

An exhausted Sheriff England provided supporting evidence: the bloody club, found where Gunn said he tossed it, and the glove.

According to Detective Reichen, Gunn also claimed that he had disposed of Miss Cotler's watch. Reichen revealed that shortly after 8:00 a.m. on December 19, he and a large search party (Prosecutor Jones, his successor Virgil Rathbun, the other St. Joseph investigators, farmer New, and others, including a *Daily Forum* reporter) had scoured the area near the schoolhouse looking for the victim's watch. After going through a fence east of the school, they spread out, walking eastward on the snow-covered ground. Then they headed north through a pasture, crossed a ravine, and turned east again to a cornfield a quarter mile away. Nothing. So, they reversed themselves and returned to the school. Finally, down a gulley thickly covered with dead grass, they found the club. Per agreement, the finders hollered to the others, who then inspected it. The piece of hedge wood, nearly four feet long, was covered with blood and human hair. But, no watch. Had it been picked up by a souvenir seeker? Sheriff England wondered how much other evidence had disappeared.

The bloody underwear found near Conception seemed to be a red herring. Likely, it was simply a rag used by hunters to protect their automobiles from bloody rabbits thrown onto the seat.

England, preparing for the preliminary hearing, had informed authorities to release other suspects. However, the feeling that he was missing something plagued the sheriff. What had he forgotten to do? There had only been two murders in the county in memory, so this was a new experience for all authorities involved.

While the *Daily Forum* could triumphantly pronounce that the state had "an ironclad case" against Gunn and residents could relax, Hattie was less certain. However careful her husband and the other authorities had been, she had heard the angry mutterings about a lynching. While the local paper had duly praised the authorities, it had also editorialized that the county could not truly breathe easy yet: "There is no place in society for fiends of such depravity." Further, it suggested that Gunn's doom should be swift.

Echoing the local paper, Hattie feared a "neck-tie party." And with good reason. On December 21, the *New York Times*, picking up a story datelined St. Joe, reported "a futile attempt to take Raymond Gunn, A Negro, from the Buchanan County jail." The Kansas City and Maryville papers offered graphic accounts of this attempt on Gunn, differing only in the details. Around midnight, a group reputedly from Maryville had assembled at Pumpkin Center, a filling station approximately twenty miles north of St. Joseph. This group, joined by what the paper claimed was one hundred and fifty others from "Maryville and surrounding towns," then motored in more than thirty cars to St. Joe. Having joined with upwards of six hundred, a crowd of eight hundred persons, most of whom were labeled non-participants, "swarmed" around the Buchanan County jail. The group, now considered a mob, tried to enter the jail through the adjoining courthouse. Unsuccessful, they had gone to the sheriff's house. They banged on the door, but did not attempt to break it down. Sheriff Roach, who had been sleeping upstairs, hurriedly climbed into his trousers, grabbed his revolver, and ran down the stairs.

He shouted to the mob that he wasn't about to open the door. Nor would he give them the keys, and if any attempted to break down the door, he would shoot the first man through. One report claimed that the mob was led by "a tall, rugged, elderly man and a younger companion," but Sheriff Roach denied that there was any leader. Instead, he recalled a disorganized mob shouting and rushing around. Another attempt was made at the jail door. Roach cut them off, again warning that he would shoot. During this exchange, Roach had summoned sixteen deputies, armed with "revolvers, rifles and tear bombs," who somehow pushed through the crowd. Simultaneously, someone informed the governor of the threat. In turn, he authorized the mobilization of the 35th Division Tank Company, Missouri National Guards there in St. Joe. The Guards' Captain Swenson phoned the sheriff that he was sending troops and four tanks, three of which were promptly stationed at corners of the block and the fourth directly in front of the jail entrance. Firemen attached hoses to fire hydrants.

Consistent with its reportorial style, the *Maryville Daily Forum*, downplaying the event, claimed the mob numbered no more than two hundred. More importantly, they emphasized that credit for the dispersal of the mob about at 3:00 a.m. must go to a "level-headed" man from Nodaway County.

The next morning Sheriff John Roach had received a call warning him that "bitter" feeling in the community portended another attempt to break in the jail. That was enough for Roach. He called the Jackson County sheriff's office in Kansas City and asked for permission to house Gunn there. By 1:20 a.m., Roach and two of his deputies had their prisoner (actually Sheriff England's) safely behind bars even farther away from Maryville. Nonetheless, the attempt to hide Gunn's whereabouts was thwarted the next day. The *Daily Forum* reported that Prosecutor Jones had talked with Gunn at the Jackson County Jail in Kansas City.

There was no letup for Sheriff England. On December 24, a warm, bright day, Hattie wrote that he drove out to the Garrett School to look for more evidence and try to prevent further souvenir seeking. That evening her husband was called out several times, including to the Gunn house, with Pete Jones. Raymond's parents, along with their friends and relatives, worried about their son. Jones and England wanted to reassure the Gunns, who were regarded as good, solid citizens, that their son would be protected. England and Jones also took the opportunity to confirm Raymond's whereabouts on the day of the murder. Thus occupied, the sheriff was forced to send Howell and one of the deputies out to make an arrest.

Sheriff England was not even spared Christmas day, though he was able to join his family for a turkey dinner with all the trimmings around 1:30 p.m.

In the wee hours of the morning, on Friday, December 26, Sheriff England and a party of deputies, including his son Howell, quietly returned Gunn to Maryville. Gunn was then formally charged with murder before Polk Township's Justice of the Peace, Phares O. Sigler.

Gunn had waived the preliminary hearing to determine whether there was sufficient evidence to warrant a felony charge. The case would go to the circuit court in Maryville on Monday, January 12, where Gunn could choose to employ counsel or have one appointed by the court.

Then just as secretively, Gunn was returned to Kansas City.

Such secrecy was warranted. Rumors of "self-appointed watchers" (vigilantes) eying Prosecutor Jones's office and house led his friends to counter with protective, day-and-night vigil. Attempts to cool the flames of revenge were made throughout churches in the county. Tightly grabbing their lecterns, clerics tried to guide those parishioners who were preoccupied by mutterings of a lynching. One preacher adopted the text, "Whosoever shall kill shall be in danger of the judgment." Mostly, it fell on deaf ears.

On Sunday, December 28, Harve and Hattie drove out to the Garrett School and visited the Thompsons, who still mourned the loss of their boarder. The Englands tried to console the Thompsons and defuse any desire for revenge. After returning to the jail, Harve listened to the radio, but did not get to relax for long. At 10:00 p.m., he was called out to an auto wreck near Burlington Junction.

The next day, the sheriff tried to ease the tension. According to Hattie, "Dad [Harve] came in at noon and said you will have to move for they are talking of putting in a new sheriff." They needed a distraction from the daily drumbeat of news about the murder. The *Daily Forum* had repeated a warning from the *St. Joseph Gazette* that neither Sheriff England nor his prisoner, Raymond Gunn, should anticipate the kind of civilized trial Gunn had received five years earlier. The recent events at the St. Joseph jail made it quite clear that it would be "perilous for any attorney to defend Gunn in court." Indeed, they "have threatened openly that if Gunn was brought [to Maryville] for trial they would 'get' the lawyer first and the Negro next."

As Harve turned in that night, he couldn't get rid of a nagging feeling. Would his friends and acquaintances turn on him? Would they give in to the violence and vigilantism that had struck elsewhere? Would his Maryville become another statistic? He would do all he could to assure that justice was done, but he had to count on the good sense of his neighbors. To Harve, Maryville was untouched by the racial violence that had consumed other areas. This wasn't the South; it wasn't even Indiana, nor closer to home, St. Joe. Still, tired as he was, he couldn't get to sleep.

The year that had started out so routinely ended anything but. Hattie's clock seemed to tick more incessantly.

Chapter Nine

"It Sure Was a Strenuous Day"

On New Year's Day, 1931, the Englands turned the calendar page and reflected on how much their lives had changed. Last year at this time, they could never have imagined such upheaval. There had been nothing to foretell the turmoil that had characterized the past two weeks. How could they have prepared for it? More importantly, how should they prepare for what lay ahead? It was quiet now, but as the time for Gunn's trial drew closer, their stomachs would surely boil.

It seemed that the whole world was on the brink of disaster. While President Hoover and his wife greeted an estimated four thousand callers on New Year's Day, unemployment lines lengthened, having doubled during the past year. Stocks had nosedived. The Chicago & Great Western Railroad shares had dropped from 25 ¾ to 17 ¾ per share; Jewell Tea had declined from 66 ½ to 38 ¾; and General Motors, which had been 187 ½ only three years earlier, plummeted to 35 ¾. Steel production, a key measure of the economy, had fallen 74 percent in just three years. Suicides, possibly brought on by the falling economy, were on the rise. The latest was thirty-five-year-old Lee Adam Gimbel, a broker and member of the family that owned Gimbel Brothers Department Store in New York City. He fell or jumped to his death, and his suicide was attributed to economic woes.

More sensationally, Adolphus Busch Orwein, the thirteen-year-old grandson of August A. Busch, President of Anheuser-Busch, had been kidnapped near his parents' St. Louis home.

At 7:30 p.m. on New Year's Eve, he had been abducted by a gunman from the chauffeur-driven limo taking him to a party at his grandfather's. (Fortunately, he was released the next day.) Again, the state of the economy was offered as explanation.

Still, some customs prevailed. The annual Rose Bowl game, with Alabama facing Washington State, was broadcast by radio. Department store sales were announced with fanfare. Women's dresses were reduced from $29.50 to $12.75 or lower. Prices of men's overcoats and one- and two-trouser suits were even more sharply reduced. Douglas Fairbanks was starring in a newly released, but forgettable, film, *Reaching for the Moon*, while Joan Crawford and Robert Montgomery were costarring in *Paid*. More memorably, the "silent one," Greta Garbo, was appearing in *Anna Christie*.

There in Maryville, the *Daily Forum* reminded the Englands of Gunn's looming court date. Virgil Rathbun, a Democrat elected in November to replace Republican Pete Jones as prosecutor, was sworn in on January 1 by County Clerk Fred Wright. The paper then made two troubling announcements. The first was not unexpected, though unwelcome: accused killer Raymond Gunn was to be brought from Kansas City's Jackson County jail to Maryville for the trial on January 12. The second announcement was totally unexpected: the family of Velma Colter "and immediate friends" had offered Rathbun the assistance of George P. Wright, who had served four terms as prosecutor. To some it sounded like they intended to railroad a conviction

The next day, January 8, the paper's headline blared that the "Gunn Case Again Dominates Talk on Streets Here." The reporters and editors wildly speculated about what to expect at the trial four days hence. For most, the verdict was a foregone conclusion, and the debate concerned whether special precautions should be taken to protect the "Murderer." "Unsubstantiated" rumors had it that the "militia would be on hand." The paper then concluded, "One thing is certain. Maryville will be a crowded place Monday...as many have signified their intention of being here for the trial."

At the same time, Sheriff England, fully aware of the talk in town, was in Kansas City to see Gunn and make arrangements with the Jackson County sheriff for his transport. On Friday, January 9, the *Daily Forum* quoted the sheriff to the effect that he "does not expect any mob violence on Monday when Gunn" is to be arraigned before Judge D. D. Reeves. Nodaway County's lawman counted on the good citizens of Maryville to "cooperate with [him] in preserving the peace." He was purposefully vague about returning Gunn for the trial, claiming that he had not completed plans to his "satisfaction yet." But England offered a gentle warning: "it never can be foretold what other damages and injuries result not alone to the defendant but to others in case of a mob outbreak. That was the last thing he wanted to happen in Maryville."

Still, the sheriff indicated that he was prepared to call out the militia "if needed," and had asked the governor to send troops. Governor Henry Caulfield ordered A.V. Adams, Adjutant General of the Missouri National Guard, to go to Maryville. General Adams was scheduled to arrive late Sunday night. In further preparation, Sheriff England had tried to confuse possible troublemakers by allowing an erroneous report to circulate that Gunn was in the Farmers Trust Company vault. Finally, he had cleared the jail of other prisoners, transporting them safely away to other jails in the county.

Hattie knew her husband; his apparent confidence was only for show. He was as worried about a mob outbreak as she.

Saturday, January 10, was a cloudy day, made even gloomier for Hattie and her ever-rotating guests by fear. The generally unruffled Hattie was sure someone must have seen the sheriff and deputies Johnny Behm and Bob Jones drive in with Gunn that dark night. Yet, there was nothing to suggest it. Gunn seemed to be safely secreted in the jail. No nosy reporters had picked up the scent, and there was no milling around outside the jail. Maybe Harve could pull it off after all. Yet, this might be the proverbial calm before the storm. There was still another day and a half to go.

On Sunday, January 11, frost covered the ground. There was no church for Hattie today. Like her husband, she was making preparations, including finding shelters for her ever-present boarders. First, she sent Doris, her crippled cousin, to stay with a friend. Next, she escorted senile Aunt Mayme across the street to the Wilsons' for the night. As she walked the short distance, Hattie stifled a laugh when she recalled her brother Joe Claypool's references to Mr. Wilson as "knocka, knocko," because of the strange noises his shoes made as he walked to and from town. Paul and Howard Qualls, the college student cousins living in the jail, volunteered to stay to help protect Hattie. Unenthusiastically, she tried to dissuade them. Ever the realist, she didn't want to take any chances. Nor did she want Harve to do so. The little bandbox jail, which had needed repairs for years, would not withstand any real charge by a maddened crowd.

At least General Adams had arrived, as ordered, and assured the sheriff he was prepared to use Battery C's .75 howitzer. However, Harve knew how long it took to position the gun, calculate a powder charge, and load the shell. Then the crew had to turn the screw and wheel to set the elevation and deflection. By that time, Harve figured, a determined mob would have overrun the small Guard unit.

Hattie was a bit irritated with one of her "guests," brother Joe. Attired in his cook's apron, he was pacing the front hall, repeating, "My God, I've got to get out of here, that jury is going to hang that man, for sure." Otherwise, she appeared calm. So far, no one seemed to realize that Gunn was in the jail. Word still had it that Sheriff England intended to drive over to Kansas City that evening and bring Gunn back just in time for the trial.

Not surprisingly, Raymond Gunn's family was fearful. Authorities promised his mother, who continued to profess his innocence, that Raymond would be protected. On the other hand, friends advised Mrs. Mildred Boone, the Douglass School teacher, not to open her school on Monday and to "go away to visit."

"Oh Boy, she was awaking morning; clear and chilly, big frost," Hattie recalled of that Monday, January 12. Despite having been up all night, she performed her chores. With the help of the Qualls cousins, she lit the stove to make breakfast for herself and others at the jail. Oatmeal, toast, boiled eggs, oranges, and coffee would get them all started properly. Alone in the big cage, Raymond Gunn was served his breakfast too. He was neatly dressed and had cleaned and brushed his shoes by the time

Hattie arrived. She gave him a bowl of oatmeal, a slice of toast, and a steaming cup of coffee with cream. Hattie asked him if he wanted an egg also. Gunn replied, "If you please," and accepted the offer of an orange as well. Despite the upcoming appearance in court and the threat of mob violence, he eagerly consumed Hattie's offerings.

Meanwhile, General Adams had mobilized Battery C of the 128th Field Artillery and issued Colt .45s. While the full complement was fifty men and two officers, it is unknown how many were actually formed for service or issued the revolvers. Governor Caulfield's instructions were for General Adams to await a call from Sheriff England, who had conferred with him earlier. Waiting in the armory, the young men were anxious. The prospect of a mob was daunting; they were without a tank, let alone the four at Sheriff Roach's disposal in St. Joseph the previous month, and armed only with revolvers and the single French .75 howitzer. Less than a block away, but out of sight of the courthouse, the Guard waited—alternately fretting or showing false bravado.

Equally anxious, Hattie's husband peered out the windows. Then, he decided to test the waters. He walked across the street and up the path to the east door of the courthouse. Except for a somewhat larger than usual number of cars and small groups milling around, it looked like any other court day. It was not unusual to observe license plates indicating folks from nearby Bethany and Albany. However, it was strange to see vehicles from St. Joseph, Tarkio, Mound City, and places in Iowa. There was also a surprising number of high school students, obviously playing hooky ("flinking," they called it), and rakishly puffing on cigarettes.

The sheriff stopped to talk to a few acquaintances. One "wag" wanted to know how they were all going to get in the small courtroom. Another playfully asked him to save them some seats.

Somewhat vacantly, the sheriff looked up at the courthouse, which he normally took for granted. It was approached from each corner by limestone sidewalks crisscrossing in great, irregular squares. The aged red brick gave the building a mellow appearance that seemed at odds with the huge, almost regal, limestone doorways on each side of the building. The steeple housing the Town Clock was visible from all four directions. For as long as any current residents could remember, its golden hands and musical chimes had faithfully marked events for them: the birth or death of a loved one, the start of a school day or business, the call to bed. It had measured their lives, good and bad.

The towering elms were now bare, awaiting the reinvigorating spring sunshine. From all outward appearances, it was just another winter day. There were more people than normal, but they weren't disorderly or particularly threatening. Instead, there were quiet conversations, a few vague murmurings about "Gunn getting his due." The Colters, Velma's parents, had quietly slipped into the courtroom to await the arrival of Gunn and the judge. Gunn's Kansas City lawyer was already inside.

As Rachel England walked out of the jail on her way to the college, she saw nothing unusual. There was a small, milling assembly on the courthouse lawn and a few people outside the jail, but she didn't recognize anyone.

Then, at about 8:30 a.m., Hattie noticed people coming toward the jail.

The first trespassers were two boys, to whom the sheriff said "nit" (nothing doing) shortly after returning to the jail. Five or six men appeared shortly thereafter and departed quite peacefully when told to leave. Sheriff England breathed a small sigh of relief and answered the call from the bailiff telling him that the judge had entered his chambers. That was the signal for Deputy Bob Jones to drive their police car out of the garage and pull up near the back door of the jail. England and Deputy Gabe Purcell then went to get Raymond Gunn. The sheriff handcuffed Gunn and, still fearful of mob violence, fastened a five-foot chain to the handcuffs and held the chain in his hand. They then whisked Gunn out the door and into the back seat of the car. The sheriff and Deputy Purcell sat on either side for what should have been a superfluous ride.

Almost immediately thereafter, nine or ten men burst into the jail and called for the sheriff. Hattie told them he wasn't there. They brusquely pushed past her to the hall in the rear of the jail where prisoners were kept. Not finding Gunn, they made a bee-line for the courthouse.

As Jones drove up to the east door of the courthouse, the sheriff must have been alarmed to see the streets becoming clogged by cars and people. The courthouse lawn was crowded too, though there did not seem to be any organization. Sheriff England later claimed that he and his deputies recognized only a few individuals. There were still no signs of violence and no threats.

Richard L. Lee County Courthouse Photographs (P0003). 3-136. The State Historical Society of Missouri, Photograph Collection.

Nodaway County Courthouse

Deputy Jones was the first out of the car. With his revolver drawn, he ordered the crowd to "Stand back, there! Stand back!" Sheriff England's sharp warning to Jones to watch out came too late; Jones was disarmed almost immediately. Deputy Purcell had barely gotten out of the car when his arms were pinned to his sides by men who approached from the rear. The more he struggled, the more roughly he was handled. Steeling himself, Sheriff England stepped out, tugged on the chain, and led Gunn out of the vehicle. Straight-backed as ever, England calmly began walking toward the courthouse, leading Gunn and asking the crowd to make room for him. But he was bluffing—the mob had the upper hand, and everyone there knew it.

This was worse than his worst nightmare. How could he have been so misinformed or unsuspecting?

To make things worse, Chief of Police Barney Dougan had let him down. Unknown to England, Dougan had been asked by someone in the mob to direct automobile traffic for it. He declined, but instead of helping the sheriff, he was in the crowd during the attack on Deputies Jones and Purcell. Afterward he lamely lamented that "there was such a push that I couldn't get anywhere near." Even worse, local patrolman William Trullinger, who directed traffic for the mob, later bragged that he had!

From behind, an unknown assailant kneed the sheriff in the middle of his back. England was forced upright, and the chain fastened to Gunn's handcuffs was jerked out of his hands. He urged the crowd to "Let the law take its course, boys," but he was met by shouts of "Let us have him! Let us have him!" Gunn, who had unsuccessfully tried to get back into the protection of the car, called to the sheriff, "Save me!" to no avail. What both England and Gunn had feared most was happening. Gunn's fate was now in the mob's hands.

Injured and fearful that calling in the National Guard would just create more bloodshed, the sheriff made no further effort to protect Gunn.

Less than thirty minutes after Sheriff England had called for the car, he was back in the jail. Joe Cornell and a couple others had carefully lifted him so as not to aggravate his already painful back and placed him in a car for the dreaded return trip. When Hattie saw him, she realized he was more sick at heart than hurt, though his back was badly wrenched.

Gunn was roughly taken to the south side of the courtyard, where the leaders of the increasingly agitated crowd discussed their plans. Though the details remain in dispute eight decades later, a tall, dark man with a weathered face, close-cropped mustache, and a short, reddish, heavy coat appeared to be in charge. Five men yanked the chain while the leader grabbed Gunn's belt, and with some help, almost lifted him off his feet. Gunn was then marched two and a half blocks south, down Market Street to First Street, where they turned right. Their westward path took them another three blocks, past Main, to South Fillmore. Ironically, now southward bound, they were headed toward Sheriff England's ten-acre farm. Their destination was the schoolhouse where the brutal murder had been committed. In the mob's twisted logic, the awful cycle would be complete.

Word of the mob's actions quickly spread. A group of approximately two hundred soon swelled with hundreds more. Reporters estimated that anywhere from 2,500 to 5,000 people eventually ringed the school. Cars began racing ahead to the Garrett School, many with hitchhikers perilously riding the running boards. Traveling faster than was safe on the narrow, rutted roads, some drivers ended in ditches.

In a three-mile march, Gunn was deliberately forced to retrace the steps he was thought to have taken that awful Monday nearly a month earlier. He was led first down the same road, and then across the same fields. He was subject to persistent questioning—and more menacingly—attacks by the crowd until the leaders encircled him. "Let this nigger alone until we get him to the schoolhouse," they commanded. Desperate, Gunn pleaded that he was only an accomplice, and that Shike Smith was the real perpetrator. But, his pleas fell on deaf ears. The would-be avengers were not to be denied their retribution.

While Gunn and his captors retraced the route to the schoolhouse, others were already at the school, and were removing desks, blackboards, tables, and the piano. Pieces of lumber were hastily formed into a ladder with rusty nails and improvised brick hammers. Two men climbed the crude ladder, and laughing, tore shingles from the roof to expose the ridgepole on which they intended to fasten the chained prisoner. From a distance, a horn sounded. A pickup truck was trying to get through the rabble. The truck stopped, and a man in overshoes, overalls, and a winter jacket emerged, hollering "Out of the way! Put out the cigarettes. Stay back." He was carrying distinctive red cans of gasoline. Others quickly took their cue, grabbed the cans, and began saturating the building with the highly inflammable liquid. As if awaiting a celebration, some others began singing, "Hail. Hail, the gang's all here."

Raymond Gunn, who had dressed so neatly, brushed his shoes to look presentable, and politely accepted Hattie's offer of eggs less than three hours earlier, was now stripped to the waist. His captors had ripped his jacket from him as they pulled, prodded, and dragged him along. Then, his shirt and shoes fell to the ground. Dust, stirred by previous marchers, had settled on his semi-bare body. Gunn pleaded for mercy, but he was met by chants of "We will give you the mercy you showed that girl."

Soon the cry went out, "They're coming." Shortly, the leaders were in sight, walking in front of their shoeless prisoner, swinging clubs, and hollering at any who obstructed their way. Walking across lots, they bypassed the cars lining the roads.

Photographers quickly started snapping pictures, but just as quickly, were stopped: "No kodaking any pictures...That's the orders." One camera on a tripod was knocked to the ground. Another photographer was quickly surrounded and his camera jerked out of his hand. A threat to break it was countered by showing the attacker that no film had been exposed. After the morbid affair, another photographer was halted on his way to his car. The men, claiming "on orders," wanted his "black box" to see what was inside. While the photographer was forced to tear up his film, others were able to preserve their images.

Shivering from fear and the raw, cold wind, Gunn was taken into the building and reminded of the killing. As if conducting a trial, questions were thrown at him until those outside began yelling for the burning to start. In what appeared to be an afterthought, the leader answered his cohorts with, "That's a good idea." Gunn was then taken outside to the west side of the building and ordered to climb the rickety ladder that subsequently broke below him. By some extra effort, he reached the top rung, still some three or four feet below the eave. With surprising agility and strength, he pulled himself up just above the edge. He was pulled the rest of the way to the ridgepole, where he stood momentarily. Forced to kneel, he compliantly stretched out to allow a chain to be attached to his waist and the ridgepole. Before he lay face down, Gunn tore his trousers off and tossed them into the crowd, some of whom eagerly grabbed for them. At 10:35 a.m., the mob leader shouted, "Let er' go." Gasoline was poured onto the roof, but matches tossed at the building were quickly extinguished by the strong wind. The aroused rabble became more agitated by the delay. More matches were lit and tossed. Then, someone fired a ball of burning paper and—whoosh—almost immediately the entire roof was ablaze. A falsetto-voiced onlooker cried out, "Goodbye, Raymond."

Photographer unknown. Private Collection.
Garrett School burning

A breeze lifted the dense black smoke to illuminate Gunn, who writhed and screamed only to be met by the crowd's jeers. For four long minutes, he suffered the torture, finally emitting what one reporter described as "a long, appalling shriek." During that torture, a woman held up her young daughter, exclaiming, "Look, honey!" An observer recalled that the mother repeated the words "bad man" to teach some kind of lesson to the child. The child attempted to follow her mother's example. Then Gunn lay motionless. Some ten to fifteen minutes later, the ridgepole and Gunn fell into the inferno that had once been the schoolhouse floor.

Then there was an eerie silence. The whole gory affair lasted approximately three hours—from 10:35 a.m., when the lit paper was tossed onto the school, until 1:40 p.m., when the fire had burned down.

After collecting souvenirs from the ashes, including two teeth out of which the gold had melted, the crowd slowly drifted away. The next morning, snow lightly covered the thousands of footprints that had marked the soil less than twenty-four hours earlier. In the snowy silence, no uninformed stranger could have guessed what an awful act had been performed there. It was as if some higher power had tried to cleanse the earth of its wickedness.

General Adams dismissed the Guard unit at 3:00 p.m., and its members mingled with friends, relatives, and college classmates who had returned from the lynching-cremation.

Tired, hurt, and crestfallen, Sheriff England faced a stream of people, ranging from reporters and photographers to his friends and family. One of the first family members was his sister Rachel Smith. Close behind was Hattie's cousin, Sheridan Graves, his wife Sadie, and their daughter Rachel. Harve's good friend and fishing partner, Les Whitehead, came and spent the night. Daughter Ruth caught a ride with one of Hattie's St. Joe friends to be with her father and mother.

Katherine Louise Clark Fletcher, a young girl when the lynching occurred, remembered visiting her aunt in St. Joe that night. At dark, there was a knock on the front door, which she regarded as unusual. She recalled,

> Pretty soon the house just seemed like it was just full of people. A doctor, knowing that [her aunt] had some extra room, had brought this family. The Gunn family, relatives of the man who was lynched, had fled the city.... This doctor had brought them to my aunt's house.... They had, I remember, two small children.

[The kids were] in shock.... They had fled [Maryville], but that is all we knew.

Over the years, Ms. Fletcher said she had learned to forgive, but feared that if it happened once, it could happen again.

Confirming that members of the black community had fled Maryville, the *Daily Forum* reported the next day that "Not a colored person was to be seen on the streets today, and it is understood that 22 of the race left Maryville."

A census reveals that Raymond Gunn's family later moved to Kansas City. Before that, Raymond's mother, who still believed in his innocence, was reported to say she felt sorry for the Colter family. However, at least they could bury their daughter; Mamie Gunn had only ashes to bury. Still, she didn't seek to avenge her son's death.

Then, for the Englands there was the blessed bedtime quiet. With only the ticking of her mantel clock to break the silence, Hattie sat down to document the day's events in her diary. She dutifully recorded many of the details, including Raymond Gunn's plea to Sheriff England to save him. She added, "God save his soul and secure it, just as he will have to secure other souls [a reference to those who had taken Gunn's life]." She concluded her entry by recalling a cousin's manner of understatement, "it sure was a strenuous day."

Chapter Ten

The Sheriff's "Trial"

For the sheriff and Hattie, the next day was "strenuous too." A St. Louis reporter was at the door before breakfast. The phone at the jail rang incessantly. Yet, wrenched back and all, the sheriff had to perform his duties. In the late evening two boys, twelve and thirteen, were brought to the jail, and an intoxicated driver from Iowa was apprehended and placed in the empty cage.

On Wednesday, January 14, a bitter cold, clear day, well-wishers presented Sheriff England with a gift, brought to the jail by Captain Tinnell of the National Guard. Others called to praise him. On forthcoming days the mail brought outpourings of support for the sheriff. One was a long letter from a prominent Kansas City lawyer complimenting Sheriff England on using his head. Another Kansan virtually echoed the lawyer's compliment, and a woman from Chicago wrote to cheer him. The sheriff patiently accepted the well wishes of more callers and was touched by the arrival of a vase of flowers, "party unknown," according to Hattie.

As if returning to normal, the rear of the jail was starting to fill up again. Two boys were brought in, fed dinner by Hattie, and released as harmless, but increasingly common, vagrants. Maybe things would quiet down, and they could get on with their lives. But it was not to be.

Editorials and reports condemning Sheriff England seemed to dominate newspapers. In similar, if not the exact, words, they

called him spineless—at best, incompetent. He couldn't hold a
candle to Sheriff Roach in Buchanan County. Roach had called
the mob's bluff, meeting it with force.

The Maryville Daily Forum *(Missouri). January 12, 1931*
Newspaper headlining the burning

A Kansas City paper seemed to want to rekindle the fiery
episode, reporting that "elemental passions" were still strong in
the community the next day. A reporter had visited Velma Colter's parents, and a "tall man," whom some readers saw as an
allusion to the leader of the mob, answered the door. He turned
to the Colters and asked whether they wanted to be interviewed:
"'No,' came a chorus from the direction of the kitchen." Hollering to be heard by this invisible chorus, the reporter asked if the
Colters felt that justice had been obtained. They answered "'Just
partly. Full justice hain't been done yet.'" The reporter alertly
picked up on the tone and content of their response and asked if
they meant getting Ted Gunn and Shike Smith too. Their reply,
"'That's it, mister,'" said it all.

The *Kansas City Times* was particularly critical. Prior to the
trial, the paper asserted, Sheriff England had assumed a "don't-
seem-to-care attitude." Afterward, he had lamely rationalized
that he had not called on the militia for fear of "aggravating the

crowd." Then, when asked how long he had been a peace officer, Harve uncharacteristically quipped, "One day too long." Nor was the reporter satisfied by Harve's defense that though the lynching was the work of no more than a dozen men, any resistance by others would only have helped the dozen "to realize their ends." Despite Prosecutor Rathbun's declaration that the mob was not from Nodaway County, the reporter pressed Harve: "Hadn't he known some of the men for a long time?" Per this account, the obviously distraught sheriff dropped his hands, groaned, and sadly "nodded in the affirmative."

The editorial concluded that Missouri had been disgraced and humiliated, the sheriff was utterly unfit, and the avengers would have to live the rest of their lives remembering the atrocity they committed.

A *St. Louis Post-Dispatch* reporter took issue with the sheriff's failure to call out the Guard. He learned that Special Prosecutor George Wright had called Sunday's pre-trial conference of himself, General Adams, Battery C Captain Ed Condon, Virgil Rathbun, and the sheriff. Wright claimed that he had suggested that the Guardsmen form a phalanx for the prisoner, with which Adams and Condon, expressing confidence in his men, agreed. But England, based on assurances that the law would be allowed to take its course, declined Adams's offer of military assistance. Further, Wright asserted that he had proposed postponing the trial until sentiment died down.

Meanwhile, *St. Louis Post-Dispatch* cartoonist Fitzpatrick graphically portrayed "The Law in Maryville" as a bloody hand.

Another newspaper took a very different tack. Rather than condemn Maryville and slap the label "mob" on "people of the community," readers should consider the lynching to be, "a determined and peaceful administration of justice." Not only lawmen like Nodaway's sheriff, but the governor as well, are at fault. They have tolerated the "banditry [hijacking, bank robbing and bootlegging] that is prospering as never before in history." If anything, the man who administered justice to Gunn should be elected governor—then America would be safe again.

Similarly, a nearby editor felt "that dirty nigger" got what he deserved. The courts had been too lenient with Gunn in the

past. He editorialized that "If the women relatives of these dam-
nably disgusting fools [apparently anyone who condemned the
lynching] were put under the mistreatment of nigger beasts
there might be a different tune to their whines, though some of
the moddycoddles could not even learn from that." Only the mob
spirit, "which occasionally flares up" will make it unnecessary to
have a czar rule this country.

And the nastiness spilled over. A week after the lynching-cremation, the *Kansas City Times* reported that a Guardsman
and part-timer at the courthouse had been fired for writing a letter to the *Daily Forum* defending "the decency of the majority of
Negroes." Worse, the reporter wrote that his fellow Guardsmen
had "amused themselves" by kicking him while he was writing
this letter.

Four Maryvillians quickly came to the town's, though not
Sheriff England's, defense. They wrote a response to criticism
from a black minister from Kansas City. They were businessman
and city manager F.P. Robinson; Chamber of Commerce president, E.W. Gray; First National Bank president, Joseph Jackson;
and the *Daily Forum's* business manager, M.W. Stauffer. In their
joint letter, they claimed that the mob consisted of the "riff-raff"
from Maryville and nearby; the good people of Maryville took
no part in the lynching.

Not even the usually considerate editor of the *Daily Forum*
defended the sheriff, labeling him a "recreant." Since the lynching, neither England nor other officials of the state had done
anything to arrest the "mob leaders." Like the businessmen, the
editor seemed intent on restoring Maryville's good name.

A scarce few papers came to Harve England's defense. One
felt sorry for him, arguing that he was "the man who faced the
trying situation—and got the worst of it." Rather than being
derelict, he did "the smart thing in not calling out the soldiers...It
would have been foolish to stir the feelings [of the hot-tempered
mob] to the rioting point." One editor felt compelled to respond
to the editors "from our large metropolitan dailies," who were
not only condemning the mob, but also demanding the removal
of the "able and efficient Sheriff, Harve England." Would they

have done differently, he asked, and risked more bloodshed by calling out the fifty or sixty National Guardsmen?

Hounded by reporters, the sheriff reluctantly offered his own defense. Painfully, he recalled for the *Daily-Forum* his state of mind on Monday, January 12. The paper reported, "Fear of bloodshed deterred him from calling on the militia to prevent the lynching of Raymond Gunn by the mob yesterday." The sheriff was quick to add that the governor should not blame General Adams for failing to call out the Guard unit: "He can blame me, if he feels that anyone should be blamed. Most of the members of the guard are young men, 18 to 20," the sheriff continued, "and I know that if they were turned loose in that crowd with automatic pistols, somebody would be killed or badly injured, and probably it would be the guardsmen." Instead, he believed he had saved lives. He reminded readers of taunts from members of the mob that "they would make short work of those 'tin soldiers,' if they came out with their 'popguns.'" Also, poignantly, he recalled that in the crowd he saw "faces that I know."

All too aware of what could have happened, the sheriff reminded the reporters that he had been in the Guard and that his two sons were once in the Guard: "I know that if they were still there, I wouldn't call the guard out; so why should I put other men's sons in such dangers; against that crowd?"

Returning to his belief in the inherent good of his fellow townspeople, Harve said that he had canvassed the town that morning before taking Gunn from the jail and "Representative men assured me there would be no attempt to take the prisoner. They deceived me. There were men in that crowd from all the towns around here." Even locals in Mound City, near the home of the Colters, had assured him "that the crowd was on hand only to see that justice was done."

The sheriff acknowledged that there were outsiders. In fact, the man who had kneed him in his back was a stranger— allegedly from Shreveport, Louisiana. The most conspicuous member of the mob, the man in the red coat, was said to be from Shreveport too. This conjecture received some support from a radio broadcast on Shreveport's station KWKH, purportedly by a "Mr. Henderson," editorializing that if Missourians did not avenge the murder of Velma Colter, they were "yellow."

Characteristically, that was the extent of Harve England's response to the criticisms publicly or privately. For him and his family, the whole, ugly episode was over; it was a closed book. But it was not to be.

On January 13, Gil P. Bourk, a Kansas City legislator, had introduced a resolution. It called on Governor Caulfield and Attorney General Stratton Shartel to conduct an investigation "to determine the cause of the flagrant breakdown in law enforcement at Maryville." The resolution was tabled on the motion of another Kansas City solon. This led to a heated debate, but at the governor's request, the speaker pro tem of the lower chamber urged his colleagues "to proceed slowly." Though displeased by the sheriff's failure to use Maryville's National Guard, the governor wanted more facts before acting. Further, he spelled out the relevant law: the county prosecuting attorney had to request the governor to direct an investigation.

Soon after, another resolution was introduced. It condemned lynching and urged punishment of any local official derelict in duty. Its target was obvious: the sheriff and Nodaway County authorities. A legislator representing a largely black constituency wanted a bill to guarantee the rights of citizens regardless of color or creed. In arguing for the resolution, the legislator castigated Nodaway County officials. This motion too was tabled.

Still in a fever to do something and fearing that tabling the resolutions would be misconstrued as disinterest, other legislators condemned the "barbarous action" of the mob in Maryville and urged state officials to bring the offenders to justice. Governor Caulfield was being pressured to do something by Kansas City's Gil P. Bourk, who represented "the most populous Negro district in Kansas City." In turn, Bourk was strongly supported by Jones H. Parker, a St. Louis Republican and former house speaker who also represented a "Negro district."

Sheriff England, the obvious target of these resolutions, was defended by Nodaway County's legislator, William Job. Emotionally, Job acknowledged Raymond Gunn's heinous crime, the equally condemnatory mob response, and the sheriff's inaction. Yet, enjoying the support of a Kansas City representative, he argued against condemning any Nodaway County officials (namely Sheriff England) "without giving them a hearing." No matter the crime, "the constitution must be upheld." To do otherwise, would be to "subject them to the same indignity perpetrated upon the negro."

An editorial in the *St. Louis Star* on January 13 condemned the inaction of Missouri's governor and legislators. It recalled the three most recent lynchings in Missouri and either the failure to investigate or the acquittal of the accused. The writer urged that another investigation should not be simply a futile gesture.

The sides were drawn, with the governor in the middle. Within hours of learning of Gunn's fate, a New York City chapter of the NAACP had telegraphed Caulfield "demanding the prompt removal of Sheriff Harve England." Black ministers from St. Joe too demanded his dismissal, as well as that of the sheriff's deputies and Adjutant General Adams.

Workers in Kansas City picked up on these protests and added a wrinkle. Issuing a broadside to "PROTEST AGAINST [THE] MURDER OF RAMOND GUNN WHO WAS BURNED ALIVE BY [A] SAVAGE MOB," they urged a mass meeting. The purpose was to defend "another Negro worker, Rudolph Gibson, who has been arrested and is in grave danger of mob violence or legal murder." A racially mixed group representing the League of Struggle for Negro Rights International Labor Defense would speak at Brooklyn Hall at an 8:00 p.m. meeting. Workers were urged to "jointly struggle against lynching, Jim-Crowism, starvation and wage-cuts."

On January 15, Governor Henry Caulfield announced that he was directing Attorney General Shartel "to make a complete investigation." Caulfield, a former congressman, court of appeals judge, and head of St. Louis's Law Department, disingenuously "theorized" that Nodaway County officers would "welcome" it. Circumventing state law, which called for an open investigation, he requested that Shartel secretly send an investigator to Nodaway County to ascertain the facts behind the mob's "defiance of the law."

Shartel had previously stated that the situation in Maryville had been such that the National Guard commander could have "overlooked the technicalities of the law to protect life and property." The attorney general also offered his opinion that "the terrible incident which occurred at Maryville should serve one good purpose; that is to stop such outrages in the future." He proposed that specially trained officers without local interest should be responsible for protecting the peace in mob situations.

Adjutant General Adams was also on the hot seat for not ordering out the Guard. A three-thousand-signature petition directed the governor to invite the Guard commander's resignation. A *St. Louis Star* editorial countered the petition by praising General Adams and recalling his successful handling of two similar incidents and a prison riot the past summer. Adams came to his own defense while simultaneously placing blame entirely on Sheriff England. He claimed that he feared "considerable danger of trouble" and had met it by mobilizing the Guard. In short, he had done all he could; it was up to the sheriff thereafter. When no request for assistance was received, he took it for granted that the sheriff "had the necessary assistance to recover the prisoner."

The sheriff's defenders vainly tried to remind others that on Friday, January 9—three days before Gunn's hearing—the sheriff had asked the governor to send troops because he was not content to rely on the inexperienced men in Maryville's armory. They also recalled that local businessmen had assured Governor Caulfield "that there was little chance of mob violence."

On January 15, a committee of St. Louis and Kansas City African Americans submitted a petition calling for an anti-lynching law and the resignation of General Adams. It had over 3,224 signatures. Four days later, Representatives Bourk and William Lafferty introduced an anti-lynching bill in the Missouri House. Punishment for lynching would be death or life imprisonment, and attempts would incur jail sentences of two to twenty-one years. Especially pointed was the bill's provision authorizing the governor to remove any sheriff or peace officer "who permits a prisoner to be taken from him and lynched or injured." The taking of a prisoner (apparently, regardless of the circumstances) was "prima facie" evidence of the officer's negligence. It also defined a "mob" as more than three persons assembled to "do violence to a prisoner in custody."

Then, just as Maryville was thrust into the spotlight, it faded. Calls for an investigation declined, and ultimately none was made by the State.

The sheriff and Hattie tried to reestablish some routine in that big, old jail they now called home. It had never really been home, now even less so. But they both had their jobs to do—for another two, long years. And it seemed that it would never be quiet there again. Something always seemed to intrude.

As if on cue, after supper on Saturday, January 17, Ruth England was entertaining Victor Mahood, whose exploits on the Bearcat football field had earned him a spot on the All-State team. Shortly before 9:00 p.m., they looked at Hattie's mantel clock, which would signal time for Vic to take his leave. It was Harve's practice to shoo away non-residents, especially male suitors, at 9:00 p.m., as he was convinced that nothing good could happen after that hour. But, he slipped up this night. Before Ruth and Vic knew it, it was 9:30 p.m., and the phone rang. Answering it, Harve must have shaken his head in disbelief and dismay.

The call was from Mayor Garrett, Hattie recalled. He had received a call from L.L. Edwards, who in turn, had gotten a call from Alice Ward, a saleswoman who had started out from St. Joe a half hour earlier. Miss Ward had reported that numbers of farmers, armed with corn knives, were on their way to town. The mayor had also been notified that the basketball game between NWMSTC and Central College had been interrupted at half-time. Subsequently he received a message that a revenge-seeking group of African Americans from St. Joseph and Kansas City were marching on Maryville. Particularly troubling, he was told that young men bearing all kinds of weapons and ammunition stolen from a hardware store were on their way.

England called each of his deputies, commanding them to "Get here to the jail as fast as you can." His next call was to the governor and then to Battery C's Captain Condon. The Guard would be mobilized, again remaining in the armory until called. Harve couldn't believe it. Not again, not his Maryville.

Harve walked to the gun case and unlocked it. "Mother," he calmly instructed his wife, "I want you to get everyone out." Then he deputized a startled Vic. In hindsight, it made sense— Vic was a member of the Guard.

Hattie hurriedly evacuated the jail of her boarders. An uncle-in-law, his daughter, and Aunt Mayme went across the street to the Wilsons'. Though accommodating as usual, the Wilsons began to wonder how many more threats to the jail and late-night visits by Hattie's relatives they would have to endure. Ruth and Rach England took Doris Mitchell, Hattie's crippled cousin, over to the Dodds'. Hattie had the longest walk, close to three blocks, to Mrs. Hartness's. As his deputies arrived, the sheriff instructed them to take the prisoners to safety elsewhere.

Stopping momentarily, the tired lawman looked out a window into the black night and assessed the situation. The sparse reports and his own observations weren't very helpful. Were last Monday's events to be repeated? A crowd of men of varying ages, visibly armed with guns, had begun to gather around the square. These self-appointed protectors were ready for the "niggers," who they believed were coming in carloads from both Kansas Cities and St. Joe.

The sheriff went outside, as he had the day of the trial. He wondered whether he could gauge the gathering crowd's mood better this time. Muffled voices professed their courage to confront the rumored mob, but unlike previously, there was no apparent leader. He recognized some of the older men, fewer than before. It was a younger group now, acting more spontaneously. Furtively, one or two disappeared, headed toward the armory. Just as furtively, they reappeared to spread whatever news about the Guard they had picked up.

Nodaway County's principal lawmen and the milling groups, spilling over from the sidewalks into the streets, waited through that long night. Every approaching car might spell the arrival of the rumored vengeance-seeking mob. None of Maryville's African American residents were anywhere in sight. Many had left town—probably less than half remained.

Once back in the jail, Harve called over to the armory. Battery C's Captain Condon, the amiable civilian druggist, also had been reconnoitering. Most of his men had shown up and loaded their Colt .45s. He wasn't sure exactly how he would deploy his men when Harve called for them. With the sheriff's agreement, he had already posted some men at the approaches to town, stopping cars and trucks to check the contents. Though Condon acknowledged that he might not have the authority, he rationalized that he and the sheriff they could rectify that retroactively.

The hours passed. Nothing. The crowd began to thin. By daylight, there was only a scattering of individuals. Thankfully, it appeared the crisis had passed.

Then, as if it were all a bad dream, there was the normal traffic on the streets and sidewalks. Relieved, Hattie, Rachel, Ruth, and Doris returned. Ruth's boyfriend Vic had been un-deputized and returned to his dorm's kitchen to "sling hash."

Over time, in bits and pieces, the cause of the scare was revealed. Raymond Gunn's mother, staying in Kansas City since her son's arrest, had wanted to return to Maryville long enough to pick up his clothing and hers. Friends and acquaintances, under the impression that she had been barred from doing so, threatened to go to Maryville to file a petition for the return of the clothes. Then the rumor mill ground out its own versions.

When he sat down that night, Harve realized how tired and sore his sixty-three-year-old body was and wondered how long it had been since he had relaxed by hunting, fishing, or playing Cribbage.

Chapter Eleven

Starting Over

Making life even more difficult, the Depression was deepening. More vagrants were being brought into the jail by Sheriff England and his deputies. On Sunday, March 22, 1931, Hattie recorded that "a strange man was brought in from near Clearmont, too dutchy to talk our language." On Monday, "our German boy came back to jail in the evening, asked to stay all night," and left a full two days later. Six weeks later, two little boys from St. Joe were brought in at midnight and bedded down upstairs in the empty women's quarters.

On June 5, the sheriff was out virtually all night. He caught a few winks and was aroused by a 6:00 a.m. call reporting a still. As he approached the area where the still was reported to be, Harve half-hoped that the operator wouldn't be there—it meant an arrest, the suspect's booking, and the start of a tiring investigation. He first had to identify the size of the still and determine whether it was for home consumption or sale (virtually all were the latter). Then he would need to gather evidence of the sales and call in the revenuers. However, this time the bubbling still and the smell wafting over the protective trees were the only evidence of human activity. So he and the deputies, somewhat relieved, performed their Carrie Nation imitation—smashing bottles.

Over the next three weeks, the sheriff was called out for a slew of car wrecks. Too often the scene left his stomach squeamish. Deaths, along with injuries requiring emergency care, occurred twice in that period. One wreck involved a young boy who was driving a car he had stolen. A deputy took the boy to the hospital for treatment, after which the young thief was jailed until sentenced to a Kansas City reform school.

Tuesday, June 9, was another trying day for Hattie. She and older son Howell were cleaning the basement of the jail when they discovered her father Byron's old law books. She lamented "too, too bad," as she and Howell burned them. She had decided that she couldn't carry the books—the last link with her imperious father—around any more. Though Hattie could put up a pretty good front, she occasionally lost her composure. This was one of those times.

On June 26, Sheriff England was out on yet another raid of a still. Beer was the brew of choice for this bootlegger. Daughter Ruth and Vic, home for the weekend, drove the sheriff and helped him dump the beer, retaining enough for evidence in the event of the operator's arrest. The following Monday, June 29, Sheriff England again brought his family on a business trip. At the ungodly hour of 4:00 a.m., he and his entourage (a deputy, Hattie, and Ruth) escorted a prisoner—obviously not considered very dangerous—to the state penitentiary in Jefferson City to serve a seven-year sentence.

Hattie had her hands full on her own—more vagrants and more NWMSTC students needing board and room in her "Inn." One was Raymond Palm, from Essex, Iowa, whom her son Howell had encouraged to attend the college and play on the Bearcat football team. Palm and another student slept upstairs in the empty women's quarters, which Hattie often used for her rotating group of boarders. A short-time boarder was an older friend from Quitman who had jury duty and didn't want to return home each night during the trial. In the meantime, Hattie baked birthday cakes for a couple of her prisoners.

The calm was interrupted on Sunday, September 20, less than a week after Palm came to board at the jail. All were ready for bed when the telephone rang for the sheriff—it was long distance. However, the sheriff was enjoying a respite, watching a movie at the Tivoli. Hattie called him at the theater, and within minutes, Harve walked in with one of his deputies. He ordered the family to "go to your rooms and put out the lights." But Hattie, who "didn't see it that way," grabbed daughter Rachel and headed to the Randalls' for the night. The sheriff, three deputies, and Palm guarded the jail the rest of that long night.

The next morning, the scare over, Hattie and Rach returned. Hattie prepared breakfast for themselves, the deputies, and the prisoners, and asked one of her "trustys" to take breakfast to his fellow prisoners. He was back almost instantaneously, hollering "we have one less for breakfast." Breathlessly, the trusty related the details: "Helpley is gone. A big hole in the floor. He sawed his way out." "Then," in Hattie's words, "the excitement began."

Upon hearing the news, the sheriff and a deputy hopped up from the table. Sure enough, Bill Helpley, who had been arrested for assault, was gone. There was nothing to do now but to call officers from other towns. Word got out almost immediately, and inquisitive visitors began arriving at the jail in numbers to see how the escape was made. One visitor was a former county sheriff, who related a similar experience years before. A phone call had led to the sheriff's and deputies' extra precautions, while conveniently diverting the sheriff's attention. Apparently, it had been placed by one of the escapee's friends. Then it dawned on them all. The mysterious and troubling phone call the previous night was to divert attention from Helpley's activities to free himself.

The sheriff's next call was to handyman Clark, who gawked at the hole, which led into the furnace room and provided access to the side door. Before the day was out, he had the hole plugged.

Less than two weeks later, Sheriff England received a call from officials in Milwaukee, Wisconsin—they had the escapee. Then there was a long train ride to pick up Helpley and what seemed like an even longer return trip. Harve wondered when all this insanity would finally end. He still had fifteen months to go.

Thanksgiving Day offered the break they all needed. Howell's Essex, Iowa, football team was playing Randolph in its last game of the season. A deputy, daughter Rachel, and Ray Palm, now Rachel's suitor, went along. It was a nice escape for the day, made even better by the home team's victory. Little Millie, Howell's wife, fixed a big holiday meal for her guests and her sixteen-month-old son, John. Palm took advantage of the trip to visit his mother, sister, and three younger brothers. Then the sheriff and his entourage returned to Maryville.

Relative calm prevailed for the next month or so, though the usual nighttime calls and routine arrests persisted. One highlight was Christmas dinner, which was prepared by two prisoners, Hattie's "trustys." By this time, few questioned Hattie's treatment of prisoners or her management of the jail. She believed jails did not have to be inhospitable and prisoners could be rehabilitated, if treated decently.

The "Year of our Lord One Thousand Nine Hundred and Thirty Two," Sheriff England's fourth—and final—year in the Nodaway County Jail, was ushered in with little fanfare. Winter had set in, which might spell a quiet time for him, his wife, and his deputies, if not for auto accidents.

A "very disagreeable morn" followed shortly. On January 4, sleet had turned to snow by 10:30 a.m. Despite accidents, or because of them, Harve asked Deputy Behm to drive daughter Ruth to St. Joseph, where she was teaching. Highway 71 was treacherous, forcing Behm and Ruth to abandon their journey at Savannah, about seventeen miles short of their destination. They then backtracked, inching their way home. Their return was met with a big sigh of relief.

Hattie would also come to rely heavily on another college student-boarder, whom she described as "manager and chief cook and bottle washer." One of her favorites, he seemed to anticipate Hattie's needs. The deepening Depression created hardships for most, but to "the Great Protector" it seemed particularly unfair to younger people. There was an increase in suicides, to which the sheriff's attention had been called. One was a student, another a young faculty member at the college. Hattie, no stranger to hardship, was troubled.

More troubling was a series of headlines in the Maryville papers in early March, which Hattie closely monitored: "No trace of the little Lindbergh babe so far." Her entry the next day, March 6, was equally sentimental: "no word from our little Lin babe. It is now 10 o'clock [p.m.] and we hope and pray for [the baby]." Two days later, she wrote, "Still no trace of little Lindbergh babe," a lament she repeated again on March 10.

Hattie was reacting like most in the United States, perhaps the world. Not even the continued fall of stock prices or the closing of more businesses grabbed the nation's attention as this calamity did. On March 1, 1932, Colonel Charles A. Lindbergh and his wife, Anne, had discovered their young son and only child missing. The two, who had been so much in the spotlight earlier, had purposely chosen secluded Hopewell, New Jersey for a retreat. Sadly, that did not protect them from either the kidnapper or the press coverage following the abduction.

The "Lone Eagle," a native Minnesotan, had become the world's hero with his solo flight from the U.S. to France five years earlier. Missourians too claimed him. Wasn't his plane called "The Spirit of St. Louis"?

Once again, though not of his choosing this time, Lindbergh was in the spotlight. Press releases, letters of advice, police, reporters, and unwanted trespassers—not to mention the baby's empty bed and blanket—haunted the Lindberghs. Then, on May 12, 1932, those awful black headlines, "Baby Dead." Harve and Hattie England were reminded of the headlines announcing Velma Colter's death and Raymond Gunn's lynching.

Hattie was temporarily distracted when her older daughter Ruth became quite sick in mid-April. Harve had one of his deputies drive Hattie to St. Joe to take care of her. After Hattie's nursing proved successful, she returned to Maryville and the jail.

Hattie's relief at Ruth's recovery was short lived. "One of the saddest things on earth happened," she recorded on April 16. Howell had called to tell her a friend had seen Rachel and Ray when they stopped in Shenandoah, Iowa. Hattie's younger daughter, not yet twenty-two and still three months from college graduation, had gone to Nebraska City, Nebraska, with Ray Palm to be married. (Over sixty years later, Rachie still wondered how Ray came up with two dollars to pay a local justice of the peace.) Hattie was crushed that they had eloped, although they later explained that no one had the money for a church wedding.

Hattie was mollified somewhat when Howell talked Ray into staying in school. Then Hattie did her part by letting the newlyweds live upstairs in the women's quarters until they graduated. Years later, Howell's wife, Mil, figured that Howell had made up for complaining when Rachel was born that "there were enough babies in the house."

Daughter Ruth and her boyfriend, Vic Mahood, followed suit and eloped to Hiawatha, Kansas, five months later. Hattie simply shook her head. At least Ruth already had a teaching job and a better rationale. School district contracts barred married women from teaching. By eloping, Ruth kept her marriage to Vic, who also was working in St. Joe at the time, secret from officialdom. Still, Hattie had been denied one pleasure—church weddings for her daughters.

Now all too often, Hattie and "the Sheriff" were alone "in the big house we call the Jail." The ticking of the mantel clock reminded Hattie of their loneliness. To fill the hours, she kept track of a surprising variety of events. On June 21, she recorded that Jack Sharkey, weighing in at 205 pounds, had beaten a 188-pound German, Max Schmeling, in a heavyweight boxing match. Though Hattie followed boxing periodically, she was relieved that Ruth's husband Vic had given up the sport. A doctor's bill for a broken thumb costing more than the winner's share for the match seemed a losing proposition. It never left Vic's system, however, and for years later he still listened to boxing matches on the radio, twisting his head and body to match the action being described. But he often fell asleep before the conclusion of the bout.

Hattie derived satisfaction from tending to the runaways being brought into the jail in increasing numbers. Hattie would feed "the scamps," put them to bed, and await the arrival of someone to take the boys home. More than a few times she empathized with a mother alternately relieved and irritated by having to come for an errant child.

Then, Howell approached Hattie and Harve. They needed a vacation, and he had just the right ticket. They could climb in Howell's Chevrolet and travel with him, Millie, and their son, John Harvey, to Los Angeles to see the Olympics! On the way, they would stop in Las Vegas, where Sam and Vera were now living. Previously, Sam had quit teaching and served as Nodaway

County's deputy clerk. He had been assured that when the clerk retired, he could have the clerkship, county politics being what they were. But, it didn't happen that way. Disappointed, Sam accepted a job as a salesman with one of Vera's brothers, who was making good money with his automobile dealership.

Howell's parents welcomed his offer. Harve had been out West before, but Hattie's only travel had been between Ohio, Illinois, and Missouri with her father and siblings. So, that July the five of them packed into Howell's Chevy.

The stop that really impressed Hattie was at Black Canyon on the Colorado River, twenty-five miles southeast of Las Vegas. At an astronomical cost of close to four billion dollars, six companies were constructing Boulder Dam, unofficially Hoover Dam. The sheer size of the undertaking was beyond Hattie's imagination. The dam eventually would be 726 feet high, greater than a forty-four-story building. She marveled at the diversity of the workers and tried to imagine preparing a thousand meals three times a day! (Her estimate was off by two thirds, for the average number of workers was 3,500.) The site was a small city, built to accommodate all the workers.

Even after marveling at the colossal dam, she was unprepared for Los Angeles and the highways, which Howell navigated effortlessly. Hattie simply could not "tell all [she saw] with pencil and paper."

Then it was back to the lonely, cold jail. Five more months to go. Slowly, agonizingly slowly, Hattie's clock ticked away. At times she willed the hands to move faster. Thirty-two years ago she had linked her fate to Harve's. Three exciting decades had passed. What would the future bring? How would they make a living once her husband left office? Would the hours pass even more slowly for Hattie without the constant turnover of guests, mouths to feed, clothes to wash, and beds to make?

The presidential campaign and election offered brief excitement. President Hoover's attempts to alleviate conditions had proved dissatisfying. Perhaps the last straw was the "Bonus Army's" march on Washington, D.C., the past summer. Veterans had streamed into Washington demanding the "adjusted compensation" that Congress had voted in 1925 to pay them twenty years hence. Shantys, better known as "Hoovervilles," had been hastily erected on Anacostia flats near the city. Hope rested with the U.S. Senate. Many veterans hung on, hoping to shame Washington's officialdom, but the promised bonuses were not paid.

Instead, on July 28, Washington's superintendent of police, General Pelham D. Glassford, was ordered to force the evacuation of the veterans. At first, as he set about the task, it was peaceful. Glassford, a retired general, had led some of these same men in France during the Great War. He was sympathetic toward them and had tried to feed and house some of them. But, tempers were short in the capital's typically muggy, summer heat. A brick was thrown. A scuffle erupted. Then stones were tossed at the police. Retaliatory shots were fired, killing two veterans. The district's commissioners, misinterpreting Glassford's statement that military aid was necessary, ordered out U.S. Army troops.

Major Dwight D. Eisenhower, aide to Brigadier General Douglas MacArthur, grabbed his riding crop, mounted his horse, and led four troops of cavalry, with drawn sabers, toward the veterans, followed by six machine-gun-mounted tanks. Behind them was an infantry column with fixed bayonets and tear gas. That evening, pausing only to allow evacuation, the helmeted soldiers fired tear gas at the defiant veterans, some of whom had been accompanied by their families. The troops then methodically burned the crude huts which had housed the protesters. The veterans fled the city.

Despite attempts to claim the Bonus Army's march on Washington was Communist inspired, it was clear that the veterans (defenders of democracy a mere decade earlier) voiced the protests of many disgruntled Americans. It was time for a change.

Many placed their hope in Franklin Delano Roosevelt, the patrician two-time governor of New York. His jaunty optimism inspired confidence, and many thought he might be able solve the nation's economic woes. The election results, giving him 472 electoral votes to Hoover's 59 (though the popular vote was much less lopsided), told the story.

And so, as Hattie's clock ticked away, the year 1932 passed into history. The jail, part penitentiary, part rooming house, and its jarring phone calls, irritating reporters, constant reminders of danger, and rotating boarders, would no longer be "home." On January 1, 1933, Sheriff England's four-year term of office ended much as it began—quietly. The long ordeal was over and the Gunn incident was seemingly behind him. Just like that, he was simply Harve England again.

His revolver would be put away forever. Why he kept it remains a mystery. Holstered, with its empty barrel, it was a sad reminder. While he had never drawn the revolver, it was a symbol—a symbol of authority, but also of failure. *His* failure. He hadn't drawn it to protect Gunn. His actions on that day haunted him—while it may not have done any good, he could have drawn his gun anyway. If nothing else, it would have been a reminder of the law he represented.

On that cold New Years Day, the Englands vacated the jail and moved four blocks south of the square, five from the jail, to the "Edwards Street house." Located on East Edwards Street, it was a two-story, wood frame house with a wide front porch on which to cool off on hot nights. It was a short walk to town, though Hattie preferred to stay home much of the time. However, this move was only temporary, as Harve planned to build a house on his ten acres south of town.

Turning over the keys to the jail meant that the Englands had to start all over again. In some ways it reminded the pair of their move to Maryville, sixteen years earlier. However, before they were preoccupied with making a home for themselves and their four offspring. Now, they were alone again, starting life anew.

For the most part, the two put the jail experience behind them and got on with their lives. Now in their mid-sixties, they were reaching the average American's longevity, though their fathers had lived relatively long lives. Hattie did wonder how people of "retirement age" started their lives over again. However, they were frugal, Harve was handy, and they had ten acres.

Building a new home and working on the truck farm—as well as hunting and fishing—would keep Harve busy. Hattie would find plenty to do, as well. She still had family, lots of brothers and sisters, though they were scattering like the wind.

Her own four were also scattering with her two grandchildren. She loved her "baby," John Harvey, who visited often with his parents, Howell and Mil. However, her other "baby," Sam's and Vera's Elaine, not yet three, was living in Illinois now.

Hattie and Harve's most pressing concern was economic. Businesses weren't recovering. Rather, recovery was stalled, awaiting action by president-elect Franklin Delano Roosevelt. He seemed to exude confidence, but that was during the campaign. Lately, his actions had been a source of anxiety—he didn't seem to want to cooperate with the lame duck president. While Roosevelt had attended a couple of meetings with Hoover, their exchanges were more like boxers sparring. In fact, an angry Hoover wanted to believe that the bank panic was Roosevelt's doing.

The panic had begun abruptly on Valentine's Day, when Michigan's governor ordered an eight-day "bank holiday" to prevent further bank failures. In the past, the Federal Reserve Bank and the Reconstruction Finance Corporation had rescued precarious banks. But now, these federal agencies seemed powerless.

Then events seemed to spin out of control. The next day, a Miamian fired on Roosevelt and Chicago Mayor Anton Cermak, missing the former, but killing the latter. Then the following day, the U.S. Senate voted to repeal the Eighteenth Amendment. Four days later, the House followed suit. Unrelated, but caught in this web of changes, other banks began to fail upon revelations that higher-ups in a big New York City bank were not only manipulating the market, but also avoiding payment of taxes. Shortly, all bankers and banks were suspect. There were runs on banks in Baltimore, leading to a bank holiday there, which spread into Pennsylvania, Ohio, Kentucky, and Indiana. By the eve of the presidential inauguration on March 3, New York State and Illinois banks were closed. It seemed unstoppable. Discredited, Herbert Hoover pronounced, "We are at the end of our string. There is nothing more we can do." And he exited from the stage. Hattie and Harve wondered what the jaunty and seemingly carefree Roosevelt could—or would—do that Hoover had not.

They were somehow comforted, if not inspired, by the President's inaugural address, as he declared that "the only thing we have to fear is fear itself—nameless, unreasoning, unjustified terror which paralyzes needed efforts to convert retreat into advance." For Hattie and Harve, both raised to be self sufficient, these words were reassuring. But President Roosevelt did not stop there. Nor did he issue more nostrums. Rather, he declared war against "the emergency" visiting the U.S.

Over the ten-day period following his declaration, there was a flurry of activity: a national "bank holiday," a tightening of controls over banking, and proposals for reducing Federal expenses, reopening banks, and legalizing the sale of beer. The new president and Congress seemed bent on restoring confidence. The big question was whether their efforts would turn things around.

Englands at Edwards Street House, 1936

Meanwhile the Englands were rebuilding their lives, which included constructing a house on their ten acres and working their truck farm. But sadly, from here on out, we must do without Hattie's delightful—and insightful—musings. Years later, daughter Rach threw away many of Hattie's notebooks, ostensibly to prevent nosy outsiders from seeing them. Fortunately, we have Harve's account books from January 1, 1940, through August 11, 1941, in which he dutifully recorded the details of everyday life: the weather, jobs performed, groceries purchased, and sales of firewood, eggs, berries, cherries, peaches, and corn. The number of eggs laid by his hens was just as meticulously recorded. One February, his eleven hens laid 132 eggs, while the next month just ten hens produced seventeen eggs per day.

England House in Maryville, 2012

Harve was just as meticulous in tracking his finances. On February 23, 1940, he recorded paying $5.04 for coffee, oil, sugar, bread, hominy, lemons, and meat. On April 20, he shelled out 50¢ for meat, 33¢ for oil, 50¢ for sugar, and $1.12 for a loaf of bread, breakfast cereal, and meat. Between September 29 and October 30, Harve sold eighty-six ricks (face cords) of firewood for $172.50. Acquiring such a sum involved backbreaking work for seventy-year-old Harve, as he had to haul the wood to his farm, cut and split it, and transport it to customers.

Harve took a break on New Years Day, 1940, to listen to the Missouri–Georgia Tech Orange Bowl football game. The next day, despite a bitter eight-below degrees, he hauled some wood. Snow fell on January 3, when he and Hattie received welcome letters informing them that Sam, Rachel, and their families had returned home safely after visiting them over the Christmas break. On January 4, Harve bucked a cold north wind to butcher a cow for a family. Braving the minus sixteen degrees, he hauled wood again the next day. The following Sunday, he butchered a hog and made sausage for the Ogdens, but lamented—to the extent he ever did—that no one came calling.

Page from Harve's Account Book 1940

Despite his new interest in football, Harve's love of baseball did not fade. That spring, he rode with Howell to St. Joe to see the St. Louis Browns play an exhibition game, and that fall listened to the Cincinnati Reds beat the Detroit Tigers in the 1940 World Series. While his Cards weren't in the Series, at least a National League team won.

Hattie remained the reliable housekeeper and continued to record in her little notebooks the events in their lives. Mostly she looked forward to visits by her sons and daughters. The daughters now had their own children—a son, Richard Wayne, born to Ruth in 1934, and a daughter, Mary Jo, born to Rachel in 1936.

Hattie prepared countless meals for family and friends, the biggest of which were for Sunday dinners. Harve dutifully recorded one Sunday when she fed daughter Rachie, her husband Ray, and their daughter Mary Jo. The next night, she fed Howell, Ruth, and their respective families—a total of eight, including herself and Harve.

Harve, ca. 1940

Freed from the jail responsibilities, the pair occasionally managed to escape from their duties. One time they rode with Ruth and Vic, then teaching in Shenandoah, Iowa, to see his parents in Savannah. A week later, Howell drove them to Quitman. At one point, they returned to their Ohio roots with sister-in-law Rachel. Then on April 10, 1940, Harve revealed that, "Mother [Hattie] had a fine birthday" for him, including dinner to which Harve had invited a friend. Then, Hattie turned around and cooked supper for Howell, Millie, and John Harvey.

On June 10, Harve recorded without comment the 5:00 a.m. departure of Ruth, Vic, and Wayne for Pullman, Washington, where Vic attended summer school. He similarly recorded their return on August 20, but failed to mention the death of Wayne's dog, Mutt, which Harve had been taking care of. Mutt had been killed crossing Highway 71 to retrieve Harve's newspaper. Mutt had been Wayne's constant companion, spending mornings in kindergarten with him and afternoons with Vic in the high school woodshop. The only time they had been separated was when Mutt was not allowed on the train for the kindergarteners' end-of-year ride to Essex, just north of Shenandoah, Iowa.

England family ca. Christmas 1939. Front row, l to r: Elaine England, John England, Robert Smith, Rachel England Smith, Mary Jo Palm, Wayne Mahood. Middle row, l to r: Ruth England Mahood, Rachel England Palm, Harriette England, Harve England, J.H. England. Top row, l to r: Raymond Palm, Victor Mahood, Samuel England, Vera Clark England, Mildred Cooper England.

Of course, Harve found time for hunting and fishing, and embarked on a three-day trip with friends to a fishing camp in South Dakota. At least a couple of times he coaxed son-in-law Vic, who had no interest in fishing, to accompany him. After all, Harve wanted company and a car driver. Not one to break tradition, for three days that September he exhibited his chickens and produce at the County Fair.

On October 29, Harve recorded simply that "Mother [Hattie] called from Shenandoah [Iowa]. Said 8lb boy for Ruth." He seemed less interested in the arrival of Gary D. Mahood than in Hattie's return on Sunday, November 10. And for some reason he did not go with Hattie when she returned to Shenandoah on December 1. He also gave short shrift to the sale of the Edwards Street house. However, he seemed excited about the rabbit hunt planned for December 4 and the Democratic Party caucus.

Harve remained remarkably healthy and fit, recording only a single instance of illness—a "touch of grippe. Home all day." And it was a rare day when he admitted to "loafing."

In his spare style, Harve recorded nothing about Hattie's health until June 24, 1941, when he simply wrote: "Our dear Mother passed away." Hattie, age seventy-two, had suffered a fatal stroke only days after she had invited her grandchildren, eleven-year-old Elaine and seven-year-old Wayne, to take a favorite item from her Whatnot stand. While the children had no idea what possessed her to offer the items, they treasured their choices. Elaine selected a pretty china vase, and Wayne took a 1909 penny, encased in an inch and a quarter square piece of glass. It helped to assuage hurt feelings from a few days earlier, when Hattie had chased him around the dining room table, trying to smack him with the straw end of a broom to punish him for some long forgotten transgression.

On June 28, Harve recorded "some clouds but no rain. Buried our dear Mother at Quitman." He would join her later in the Odd Fellows cemetery. Fortunately, daughter Ruth, Vic, and their sons were staying with him and offered support. Thirteen days later, Harve entered his last item in his account book.

Just short of four years after Hattie's death, Harve passed away at age seventy-seven—forty-five years to the day after he and Hattie had wed. Lonely after her death, he had gone to Washington State and had married an old friend, much to his older daughter's chagrin.

Harve's and Harriette's graves in Odd Fellows cemetary, Quitman, MO

Some seven decades later, Hattie's and Harve's little two-bedroom house remains, and Hattie's mantel clock ticks on. The Englands, caught up in the aftermath of two horrific crimes, are barely footnotes in history. Still, their story is a reminder that the "good old days" had a very dark side—a side from which we can never be wholly free.

Epilogue

The ugly episode of early 1931 would haunt the Englands the rest of their lives. Yet, publicly it was a closed book—the subject was too painful. While rarely mentioned, the sons nevertheless saved the newspapers with the gruesome details about the lynching-cremation. The memory would forever be a part of them. These newspapers, along with Hattie's notebooks, were hidden until well into my adulthood when I began asking questions. Little by little, information came forth, and somehow I became the family repository. It began with artifacts, ephemera, scrapbooks filled with photos, a newspaper item or two, letters, and then Hattie's notebooks that my mother shared with me. After that, I made a determined effort to learn all I could about the lynching. Then, for another two decades, it took a back seat to family, job, and other interests.

So, why dig up the past? When Alison Light traced her family in *Common People*, she asked, "Why does the past matter? How much do we owe the dead?" As I learned and wrote about my grandparents, I found myself asking the same questions. With each discovery, especially Hattie's notebooks, it became more personal. Where did I come from? How does the past relate to me? While Harriette Claypool and her husband Harvey England were my grandparents, I found I really didn't know them. Immersing myself in the documents of their daily lives, I understood what Alison Light meant when she wrote, "family historians are resurrectionists, repopulating the past, trying to put flesh to bones and bring past eras to life."

Harve was easily the most difficult to "resurrect." He remains distant—he would never be the familiar "Papa" or "Grandpa." Well into her nineties, daughter-in-law Mil still referred to him as "Mr. England." Yet, her son recalls comfortably sitting on his grandfather's lap and asking questions about scars on his hands. Harve's own account book revealed a man who apparently hid his emotions. Several factors may have contributed to his reticence: the death of his mother when he was relatively young, his father's seeming lack of guidance, or his experiences when he was on his own in Washington Territory. Calling Hattie "Mother" may have been as close as he came to showing his feelings. Yet, looking back on myself when I was his age, I realize how capable he was—making a living on a ten-acre truck farm was no small task. Harve's meticulous record of his daily activities demonstrate a remarkably resourceful man: hauling and ricking wood, butchering hogs and cows, rendering lard, and braving temperatures below zero and higher than one hundred degrees Fahrenheit. Not to mention, he was able to garner respect and esteem almost from his arrival in Maryville.

Nor was Hattie all that demonstrative. Yet, people were comfortable with her—she cared for others, and it was obvious. Though she died when I was relatively young, she is real to me. Of course, my mother's memories of her have given me insight into her character, but nothing is as revealing as her detailed notebooks. I'm reminded of her interest in heavyweight boxing, poking fun at stuffed shirts, and her delightful, understated sense of humor.

Her musings, written before she went to bed, captured the day's events that were interesting or important to her. Generally, what she wrote was brief, at times cryptic, and commonly bared her feelings. For example, on Wednesday, December 16, 1931, she wrote, "one year ago this evening a horrible murder was committed at Garrett School house: our little Girl Velma Colter."

I also came to appreciate and know my mother and her siblings better. If anything, I realized I had taken my mother for granted. She was not just my mother and a well-respected teacher, but also had been a pretty good athlete, excellent student, and class leader. Letters to and from her brothers and sisters also revealed their strengths and achievements, of which I was unaware or had taken for granted. Howell, particularly, comes through as a thoughtful son, brother, husband, and father.

While, sadly, my grandfather remains nearly as distant now as he was when I saw him as a gray-haired, stiff backed, crown-hatted older man, just like that I'd grab Hattie, the "Great Protector," and give her a big hug.

Much as Harve and Hattie tried to put the jail episode away, periodically the Gunn lynching is recalled. Twenty years ago it was the topic of a Master's thesis at Maryville's Northwest Missouri State University. A quarter century before, novelist MacKinlay Kantor devoted a chapter to the story, castigating Sheriff England and rousing the ire of a Battery C member who wrote:

> What effect could we Guardsmen, untrained in riot control and ill-equipped…have against a mob of the proportion that ultimately gathered that day? If the governor and General Adams were so concerned, why didn't they order out the tank company from St. Joe?…Incidentally, they failed wretchedly only four years later in a similar incident; not even a shot was fired while a black man was cruelly mutilated…And why the attack on Sheriff England, a compassionate man, who enjoyed the respect of the community, and knew the situation better than anyone?

He was referring to a lynching in St. Joe, just four years after Gunn was barbarically murdered. Again, it was sparked by the alleged murder of a white girl by a black man. Around noon on the day of the trial, a crowd gathered outside the jail. The National Guard unit was called out with four tanks, one of which the mob captured and used to rip off the two doors of the new, reputedly escape-proof jail. As with Gunn, the frenzied mob dragged the prisoner before mutilating, hanging, and burning him. The Buchanan County sheriff was no more able to thwart a mob than Sheriff England.

However horrific such incidents are and however much the Englands and others tried to forget, racism and extralegal means to avenge wrongs are not just relics of the past. In resurrecting this incident and my connection to it I realized that it might relate to others. Telling the Englands' story might offer insight into the broader American experience. Bridging two centuries, Hattie and Harve were touched by some of the most defining experiences in American history: the Civil War, homesteading, Prohibition, the "Roaring Twenties," the Great Depression, and racial violence, to name a few. Furthermore, the Englands' story explores the experiences of everyday rural life otherwise overlooked in the historical record: for example, the struggle to make a living, the engagement in community, and the favorite entertainments or pastimes. Perhaps most importantly, the Englands were witnesses to an otherwise overlooked and anomalous atrocity—a lynching in a quiet Midwestern town. In the suddenness and horror of the lynching, the insidious nature of racism and collective violence is revealed, and the England's horrible memory takes on a broader historical and social relevance.

Finally, this may serve as a reminder that every family has a story to tell.

Bibliography

Manuscripts and Correspondence

Claypool, Byron. *Letters.*
England, Elizabeth Ann. *Letters.*
England, Harve. *Letters.*
_____. *Account Book.*
England, Harriette. *Diary.* 1917-1940.
England, J.H. *Letters to the author and reminiscences.*
England, Jesse. *Letters.*
England, Samuel. *Letters.*
Lamb, Mabel Collins. *Letters to the author.*
Mahood, Ruth England. *Letters to the author and reminiscences.*
May, Walter. *Letter to author.* February 4, 1971.
_____. *Letter to J.H. England.* December 19, 1970.
_____. *Letter to J.H. England.* December 20, 1970.
Palm, Rachel England. *Reminiscences, letters, and phone calls with the author.*
Smith, Walter. *Letter to author.* January 22, 1971.
Yarborough, Harold. *Letter to Walter May.* n.d.

Newspapers

Chilcotte, Merrill. "Timely Observations: A Letter Unprinted for 50 Years." [n.d., but it appears to have been printed in

the 1980s in the *St Joseph News Press*, of which Chilcotte was an editor from the 1930s into the 1980s.]
Kansas City Times, December 22, 1930-January 29, 1931.
Kansas City Star, December 18, 1930-January 14, 1931.
Literary Digest, January 31, 1931.
Maryville Democrat-Forum (Missouri), May 1919-June 1941.
New York Times, December 22, 1930-November 8, 1933.
Outlook & Independent, January 28, 1931.
St Joseph Gazette (Missouri), December 17, 1930-January 13, 1931.
St. Joseph News Press (Missouri), December 17, 1930-February 7, 1931.
St. Louis Post-Dispatch, December 17, 1930-January 25, 1931.
St. Louis Star, January 12-13, 1931.

Books

Ames, Jessie Daniel. *The Changing Character of Lynching*. Atlanta: Committee on Interracial Cooperation, 1941.
Cooper, Martha L. *Life, Liberty and the Pursuit of Happiness: Nodaway County Missouri, A Black History 1840-1940*. Maryville, Accent Printing, 1992.
Croy, Homer. *West of the Water Tower*. New York: Grosset & Dunlap, 1923.
Danzig, Allison. *The Greatest Sports Stories from the New York Times*. New York: Barnes, 1951.
Dyer, Frederick. *Compendium of the Civil War*. Des Moines: Dyer Publishing, 1908.
Huber, Patrick J. and Gary P. Kremer. "Raymond Gunn." In *Dictionary of Missouri Biography*, eds. Lawrence O. Christensen, William E. Foley, and Gary Kremer, 359-361. Columbia: University of Missouri Press, 1999.
Kantor, MacKinlay. *Missouri Bittersweet*. Garden City: Doubleday & Lancaster, 1969.
Lancaster, Bob and B.C. Hall. *What Really Happened on July 10, 1981?* New York: Putnam, 1983.
Light, Allison. *Common People: The History of an English Family*. London: Fig Tree, 2014.
Lord, Walter. *The Good Years*. New York: Harper & Brother, 1960.

Madison, James S. *A Lynching in the Heartland: Race and Memory in America.* New York: Palgrave, 2001.

Mahood, Wayne. "Hattie." *Tales of Nodaway County.* Maryville: Nodaway County Historical Society, 1977.

Raper, Arthur F. *The Tragedy of Lynching.* Chapel Hill: University of North Carolina Press, 1933.

Waers, C.F. "Horror at the Schoolhouse." In *The Master Detective.* September 1935, 6-12, 56-58.

White, Walter. *Rope and Faggot: A Biography of Judge Lynch.* New York: Knopf, 1919.

Miscellaneous

Armstrong, Orland Kay. *The Lynching at Maryville: A Case Study.* Atlanta: Southern Commission on the Study of Lynching, 1931. Howard Washington Odum Papers (#3167), Southern Historical Collection, University of North Carolina Chapel Hill.

Claypool, Byron. Military Service Record and Pension Papers, National Archives.

Eagle Bytes.

England, Harve. Obituary.

England Jesse. Military Service Record and Pension Papers, National Archives.

"Klu Klux Klan History." *Anti-Defamation League.* Web.

"Lynching in America: Statistics, Information, Images." *University of Missouri-KansasCity.* Web.

Maryvillian (Northwest Missouri State College Yearbook), 1927-1928.

Index

A

Ackerman, "Aunt Mayme" 86, 116, 136
Adams, Adjutant General A. V.
  dismissal called for 133
  dismissed Guard unit 124
  England defended 131
  mobilized Battery C in Maryville 115–116
  pre-trial conference 129
Alexander, Grover Cleveland 67
Andrews, Detective B. T. 102, 104
Atherton, Leo
  brought Gunn in for questioning 103

B

Bacon, "Widow" 8, 24
Bald Knobbers 94
Barnum, P.T. circus 38
Battery C, 128th National Guard 40, 56, 81, 82, 88, 101, 116, 135, 159
Behm, Johnny
  appointed as deputy 88
  drove Ruth England to St. Joe 142
  pictured 90
  transported Gunn 115
Bilby, John S. 8
Bilby Ranch 8, 21, 23
Black Bombers 22
Boone, Earnest
  Douglass School principal-teacher 35
  service in WWI 40
Boone, Mildred
  advised to close Douglass School 116
  Douglass School principal-teacher 35
Bourk, Gil P.
  introduced anti-lynching bill 134
  introduced resolution for investigation 132
Brown Brothers 24
Brown, Willie
  murder of 42
Bryan, William Jennings 25
Burlington Junction, Missouri 6, 14, 31, 41, 53, 61, 71, 111
Burnett, Detective Tom 102, 104

C

Caldwell, Sarah 30
Campbell, Lowell B.
  appointed England as deputy 59
  apprehended moonshiners 61, 74
  filed candidacy for county sheriff 57
  term as sheriff 65, 78
Camp Dennison, Ohio 17
Carnegie, Dale 30
Carnegie Free Library 39, 41
Caulfield, Governor Henry

called on to investigate lynching
132
directed Attorney General Shartel
to invesigate lynching 133
ordered Guard to Maryville 115,
117
Childress, H. P. 41
Chillicothe, Ohio 13
Claypool, Byron vii
death 52
early history 5
Claypool, Dora vii, 6, 81
pictured 7
Claypool, Elizabeth (Graves) vii, 5
death 6
Claypool, Isaac vii, 6
Claypool, Spencer vii, 6
Claypool, Theodosia "Dosia" 6
pictured 7
Colter, Velma Fern
funeral 106
murder 99–103
Columbia River 18
Condon, Captain Edward 88, 129,
135
Coolidge, President Calvin
sworn in 53
Cornell, Joe 120
Corvallis, Oregon 18
Croy, Homer 30

D

Davis, Coach "Lefty" 92
Dean, Jerome "Dizzy" 92
Dempsey, Jack 67
Douglass School 40, 105, 116
Duncan, Detective John T. 102

E

Earhart, Amelia 77
Eisenhower, Maj. Dwight D.
role in evicting the "Bonus Army"
146
Electric theater 37, 45
Empire theater 37, 45

England, Clarinda Jane "Clara" 11,
13, 19
England, Edward 10
death 13
England, Elaine 148, 154
birth 91
pictured 153
England, Eliza Ann vii, 11–13
death 13
England family photograph , 67, 27,
149
England, Harriette "Hattie" (Claypool)
attended Sam's athletic events 71
burned father's law books 140
care of father and father-in-law 28
childhood 5–8
courtship with Harve 23
death 154
diary vii–ix
early marriage 23–27
emptied jail of non-inmates
115–116
fed Gunn breakfast 117
followed boxing 144
met Harve England 9–10
move to Maryville 31
recalled Colter's murder 158
traveled to 1932 Olympics 144
trip to Ohio 152
unexplained illness 81
vacated the jail 147
visited the Thompson family 111
England, Harvey "Harve"
accepted blame for failure to order
out Battery C 131
appointed as chief of police 55
appointed deputy 60
appointed night watchman 49
apprehended moonshiners 64, 74
April 1st fishing trip 47
attacked by mob outside courthouse 120
attended Sam's athletic events 71
captained baseball team 22
childhood 11–15

criticism of 127–131
death 154
elected president and superintendent of the Northwest Missouri Poultry Association 43, 58
elected sheriff 83
expanded farm 63, 74
filed candidacy for county sheriff 57, 80
first marriage and divorce 18
hired at Bilby ranch 21
homesteaded in Washington Territory 16–19
led investigation of Colter's murder 101
lost election 57
managed truck farm 36, 51
met and married Hattie 23
moved to Maryville 31
notified of Colter's murder 99
opened ice plant 41
pictured 22, 46, 64, 67, 152, 153
Quitman baseball team 21
returned Gunn to Kansas City 111
revived Izaak Walton League 74
saved restaurant from fire 49
"special policemen" 58
traveled to 1932 Olympics 144
trip to Ohio 152
vacated the jail 147
visited Sam in Las Vegas 144
visited the Gunn family 111
wagon accident 19
England, Jesse
death 28–29
early history 10–15
homesteaded in Washington Territory 16–19
moved to Quitman, Missouri 14
pictured 11
England, Jesse Howell "J.H."
April 1 fishing 47
birth 26
buggy accident 50
college graduation 63
eloped with Mildred Cooper 72

high school athletic letter 50
high school graduation 51
led cow to Maryville 31–33
Missouri National Guard 55
National Guard summer camp 72
NMSTC "M" Club induction 55
pictured , 67, 27
school play 51
served as principal in Fortescue, MO 66
trip to 1932 Olympics 144
England, John Harvey
born 91
pictured 153
England, Mary Alice
death 11
England, Mildred "Millie" (Cooper)
eloped with J.H. England 72
hosted Thanksgiving 141
pictured 153
England, Rachel. *See* Smith, Rachel (England)
England, Rachel Elizabeth. *See* Palm, Rachel "Rachie" (England)
England, Ruth. *See* Mahood, Ruth (England)
England, Samuel Herman
April 1 fishing 47
attended Washington School 34
birth 26
eloped with Vera Clark 72
graduation from NWMSTC 63
high school athletic letter 50
high school graduation 51
led cow to Maryville 31–33
"M" Club Hall of Fame 59
Missouri National Guard 55
move to Las Vegas 144
National Guard summer camp 72
pictured , 67, 27
taught and coached at Savannah High School 66
England, Vera (Clark)
eloped with Sam England 72
pictured 153
Essex, Iowa 140, 141, 153

F

Field, Henry 58
First Baptist Church 38
First Christian Church 38
First Presbyterian Church 38
Fletcher, Katherine Louise Clark 124

G

Garfield School 34, 50
Garrett, Mayor W. O. 74
    appointed Harve England chief of
        police 55
    warned Sheriff of possible mob
        135
Garrett School 99, 107, 111, 121, 158
Gehrig, Lou 68, 73
Gimbel, Lee Adam 113
Glassford, General Pelham D. 146
Glidden, Joseph 21
Graves, Eliza 24
Graves, Rachel 124
Graves, Sadie 124
Graves, Sheridan 124
Gray, E. F. 49, 130
Great Depression 92
Gunn, Adolphus
    drafted in WWI 40
Gunn, Gilbert Emmett "Em" 35
    fled Maryville 124
    visited by Sheriff England 111
Gunn, Mamie (Finley) 35
    fled Maryville 125
    visited by Sherff England 111
Gunn, Raymond
    brought in for questioning 104
    brought to courthouse for trial 118
    captured by mob 120
    early history 105
    formally charged with Colter's
        murder 111
    held in Buchanan County jail 109
    murdered at Garrett School 122
    pictured 106
Gunn, Sam 35
Gunn, Ted 104, 128

Gunn, Violet 35, 40
    oral history 35

H

Harding, President Warren 53, 63
Holmes, Ned 40
Hoover, President Herbert 83, 87,
    113, 145, 146–148
Humberd, Dr. Charles D 99–101,
    103, 105
Hundred and Two River 15

I

Iba, Henry 30
Independent Order of the Odd Fel-
    lows (IOOF) 23
Indian Creek, Ohio 12, 13
International Workers of the World
    (IWW) 42

J

Jackson, Joseph 130
James, Frank 94
James, Jesse 94
Jewell, William 36
Johnson, Rev. William M 42
Jones, Paul "Pete" 83, 100–105, 108,
    110–111, 114–115
Jones, Robert 88
Jones, Warren 30, 37, 91

K

Kalama, Washington 18
Kansas City, Missouri 15, 26, 70, 78,
    79, 110, 111, 114, 116, 125,
    128, 132, 134, 137
Kantor, MacKinlay 159
Knox, L. Amasa
    represented Raymond Gunn 97
Kuchs, Paul 71
Ku Klux Klan 53, 55, 97

L

Lafayette, Indiana 5
Lawrence, Lt. H.F. "Shorty" 101
League of Nations 42, 53
Lindbergh, Charles
  baby kidnapped 142
  flight across the Atlantic 72
Louisville, Kentucky 17
Lynch, Colonel Charles
  credited with first lynching 94

M

MacArthur, Douglas 146
Mahood, Gary
  birth 154
Mahood, Richard Wayne
  birth 151
  pet dog killed 153
  pictured 153
Mahood, Ruth (England)
  attended Washington School 51
  birth 26
  college activities 72, 83
  eloped with Victor Mahood 144
  high school activities 60
  high school graduation 66
  pictured , 67, 27
  rode with sheriff on raid 140
Mahood, Victor
  deputized 136
  drove sheriff on raid 140
  eloped with Ruth England 144
  football 73, 92
  pictured 153
Maitland, Missouri 22, 26
Malcolm, James 42
Marmaduke, Governor John S. 29
Maryville High School 54, 73, 100
Maryville, Missouri
  businesses 36–38
  in 1916 29
  schools 33–35
May, Earl 58
McKechnie, Bill 91
McKinley, President William 25

McMillen, C. G. (Grant) 88
  pictured 90
Methodist Episcopal Church 106
Missouri National Guard 56, 115
Missouri Theater 66
Mitchell, Doris 86, 136
Morehouse, Governor Albert P. 29
Morristown, Indiana 5

N

Nashville, Tennessee 17
Nation, Carrie 25, 139
New York Yankees 68, 73
Nodaway River 14, 15, 21
Northwest Missouri Poultry Associa-
  tion 43, 58, 88
Northwest Missouri State Teachers
  College 53, 54, 97

O

Oak Hill Cemetery 36
Omaha, Nebraska 23, 35, 42, 58, 66,
  79, 105
Orwein, Adolphus Busch 113

P

Palmer, Attorney General Mitchell
  41
Palm, Mary Jo
  birth 151
  pictured 153
Palm, Rachel "Rachie" (England)
  attended Garfield School 50
  birth 26
  Elizabethan Literary Society 60
  eloped with Raymond Palm 143
  exhibited chickens 44
  high school activities 60, 84
  high school graduation 81
  pictured 67, 153
  trial day 118
Palm, Raymond
  boarded at the jail during college
  140

eloped with Rachel England 143
pictured 153
visited mother with the Englands
141
Parshall, Lulu 28
Peone Prairie, Washington Territory
16
Perkins, Clyde "Fatty" 91
Prohibition 63, 77

Q

Quantrill, William 94
Quitman, Missouri 14, 15, 16, 21,
155

R

Rasco, Deputy John 61, 74
Rathbun, Virgil 101, 108, 114, 129
"Red Scare" 41
Reichen, Detective John 102, 104,
105, 107
Ribeau, Louis 93
Rickey, Branch 91
Rimel, George 88
Roach, Sheriff John 109, 117, 128
Robinson, F. P. 130
Roosevelt, Franklin Delano 146,
148–149
Roosevelt, Theodore 25
Ruth, George Herman "Babe" 68, 73

S

Sacco and Vanzetti case 72–73
Savannah, Missouri 54, 66, 71, 92,
97, 101, 152
Scio, Oregon 18
Shartel, Attorney General Stratton
132–134
Shenandoah, Iowa 58, 101, 143, 152,
153
Sisson, Nathaniel 41
Smith, Arthur 40
Smith, Delilah (England) 12, 14
Smith, George 12, 14

Smith, Governor Alfred "Al" 83
Smith, Paul "Shike" 104, 121, 128
Smith, Rachel (England)
birth 11
married Robert Smith 16
pictured 17, 153
visited Englands after the lynching
124
work at millinery store 9
Smith, Robert
blacksmith business 9
lent money to Harve 25
married Rachel England 16
pictured 153
Southworth, Billy 91
Spanish Flu 40
Spokane, Washington Territory 16
Stauffer, M.W. 130
St. Gregory's Church 38
St. Joseph, Missouri 52, 65, 79, 92,
97, 102, 104, 107, 108, 117,
135, 142
St. Louis Cardinals 58, 91
St. Mary's Church 38
Strumphfer, H.G. 102
Surplus, John 80

T

Teapot Dome scandal 63
Thompson, T.H. 99, 105
Tillman, Senator Benjamin 95
Tilton, Chief E. E. 49
Toulon, Illinois 6
Tunney, Gene 67
Turner, Charley 24

U

United Mine Workers strike 41
U.S. Highway 71 79

W

Walter, Harvey 57
Ward, Alice 135
Ward, Paul 99

Washington School 34, 50
Washington Territory 10, 16, 19, 158
Weddle, James Wallin 16
Whitehead, Les 124
Williams, Virgil "Virg" 86–87
Wilson, President Woodrow 42
World Series
   1926 68
World War I 40
Wright, County Clerk Fred 80, 114
Wright, George 74, 129

www.ingramcontent.com/pod-product-compliance
Lightning Source LLC
Chambersburg PA
CBHW070806050426
42452CB00011B/1919